LADY STUFF

ALSO BY LORYN BRANTZ

Feminist Baby
Not Just a Dot
Harvey the Child Mime

LADY STUFF

Secrets to Being a Woman

LORYN BRANTZ

Andrews McMeel
PUBLISHING®

LADY STUFF

Andrews McMeel Publishing
a division of Andrews McMeel Universal
1130 Walnut Street, Kansas City, Missouri 64106

www.andrewsmcmeel.com

17 18 19 20 21 SHO 10 9 8 7 6 5 4 3 2 1

ISBN: 978-1-4494-8677-8

Library of Congress Control Number: 2017936377

Editor: Allison Adler
Art Director: Holly Swayne
Production Editor: Maureen Sullivan
Production Manager: Carol Coe

ATTENTION: SCHOOLS AND BUSINESSES

Andrews McMeel books are available at quantity discounts with bulk purchase
for educational, business, or sales promotional use. For information, please e-mail the
Andrews McMeel Publishing Special Sales Department:
specialsales@amuniversal.com.

GROOMING AND HABITAT MAINTENANCE

IT IS IMPORTANT TO LOOK YOUR "BEST" IN ANY LIGHT.

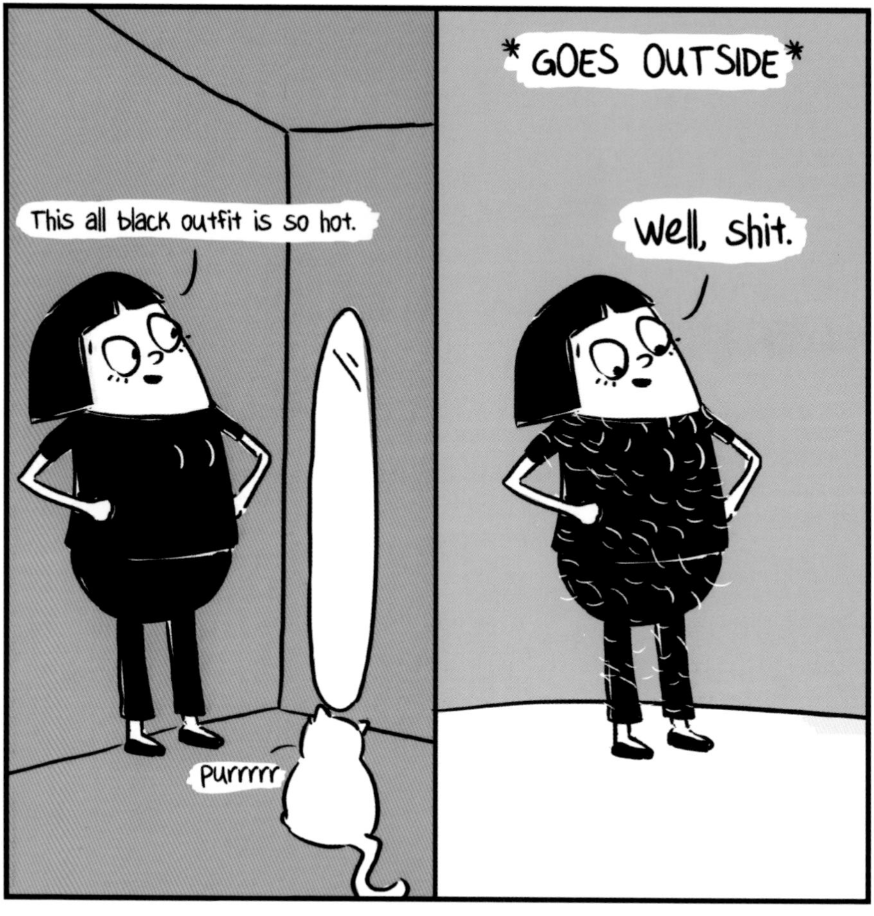
This all black outfit is so hot.
purrrrr
GOES OUTSIDE
Well, shit.

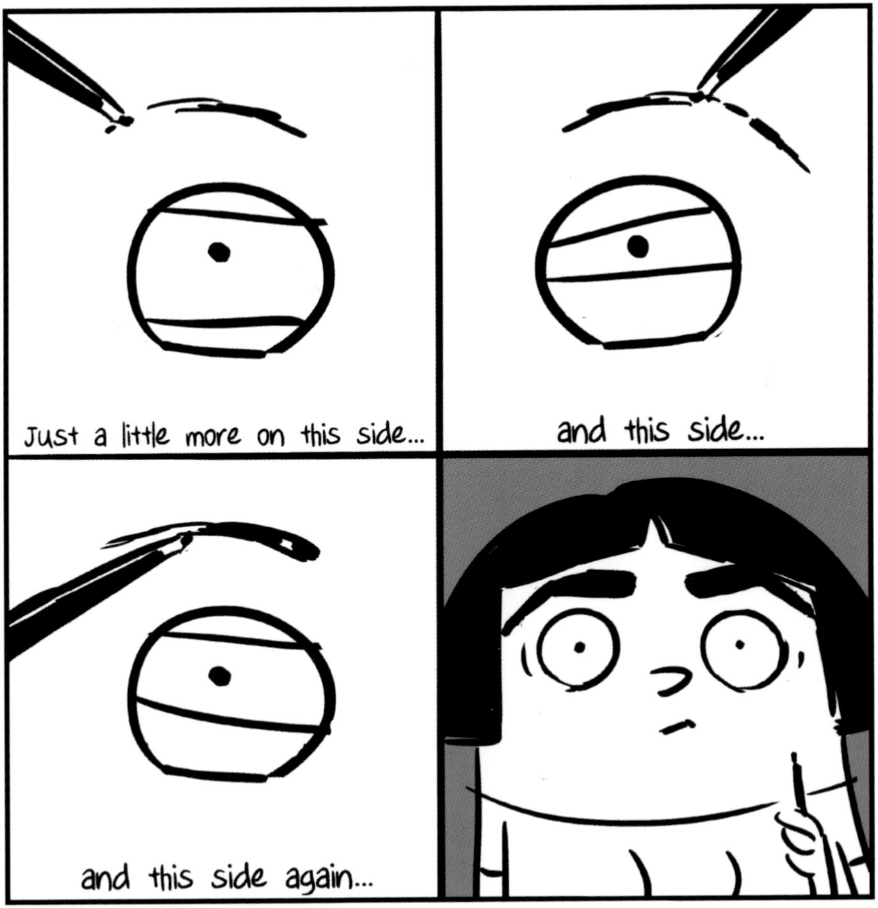
Just a little more on this side...
and this side...
and this side again...

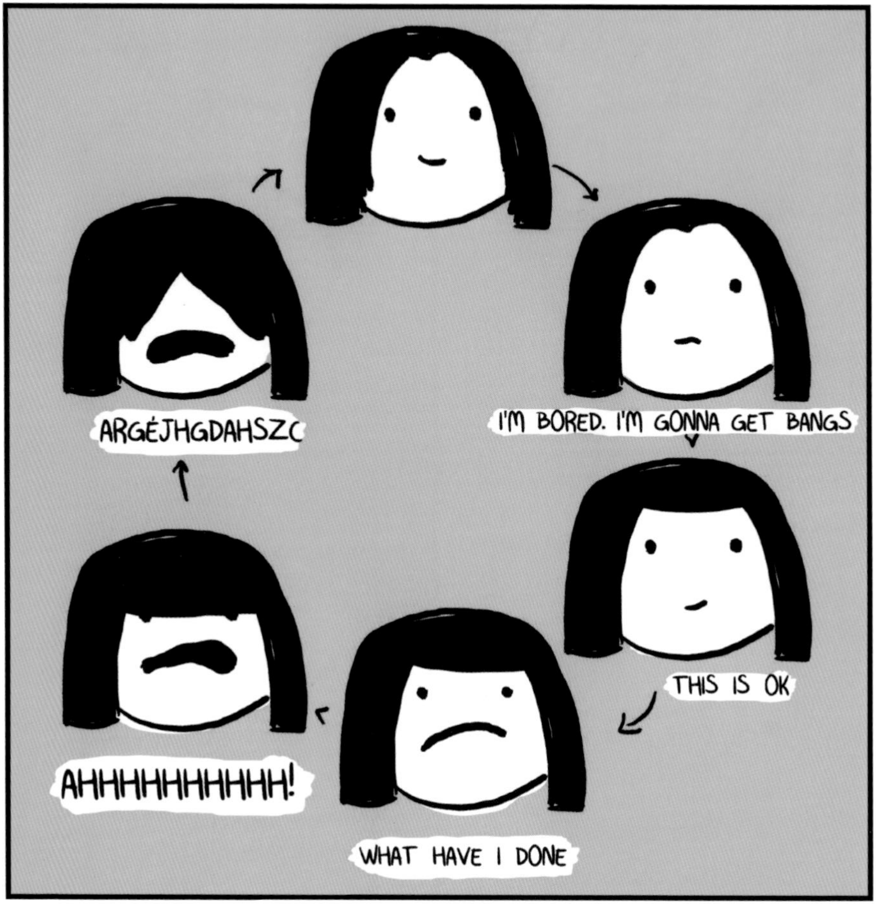
I'M BORED. I'M GONNA GET BANGS
THIS IS OK
WHAT HAVE I DONE
AHHHHHHHHHH!
ARGÉJHGDAHSZC

ALSO, KEEP YOUR EXPECTATIONS IN CHECK.

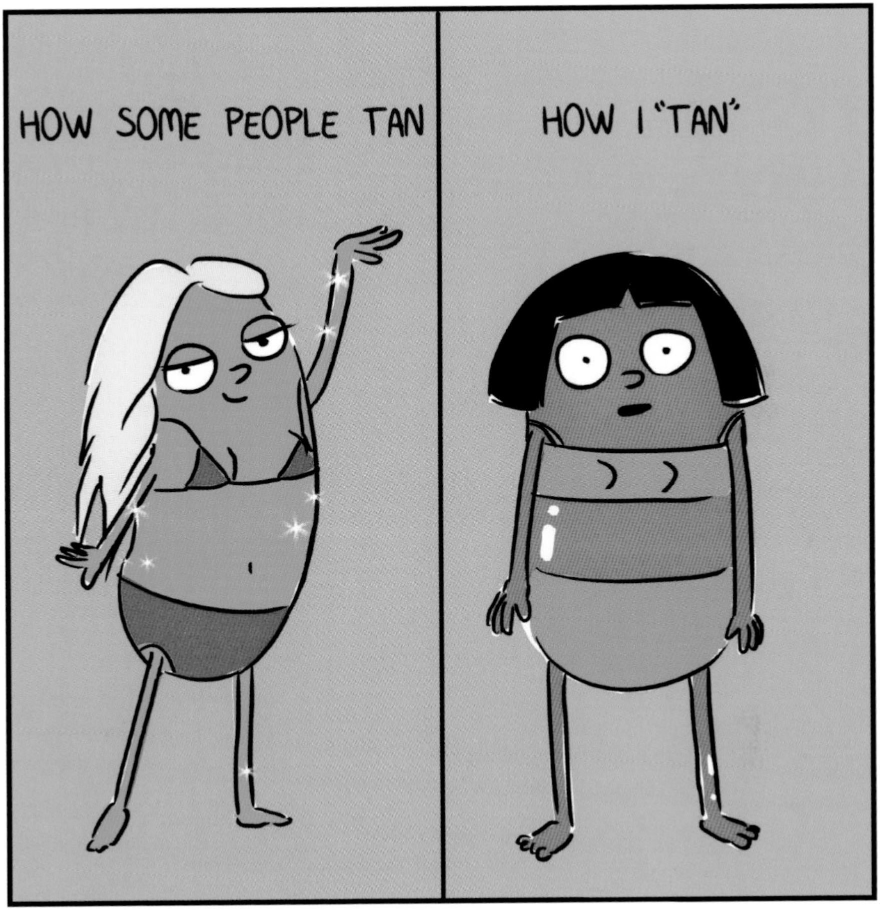
HOW SOME PEOPLE TAN
HOW I "TAN"

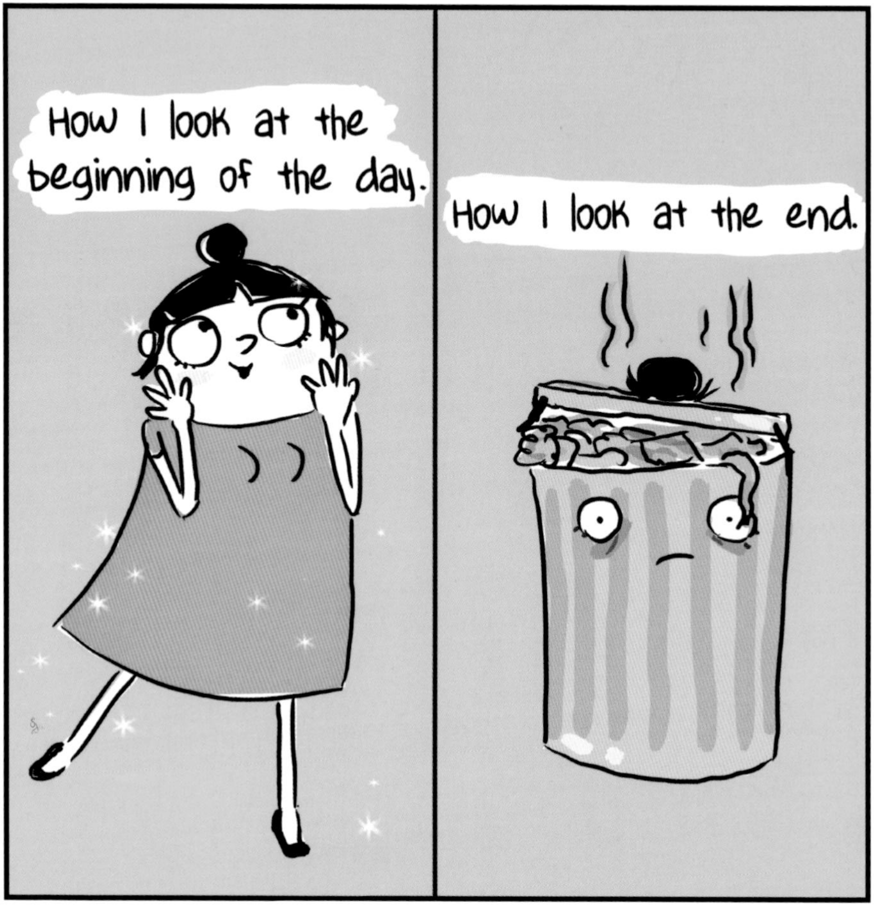
How I look at the beginning of the day.
How I look at the end.

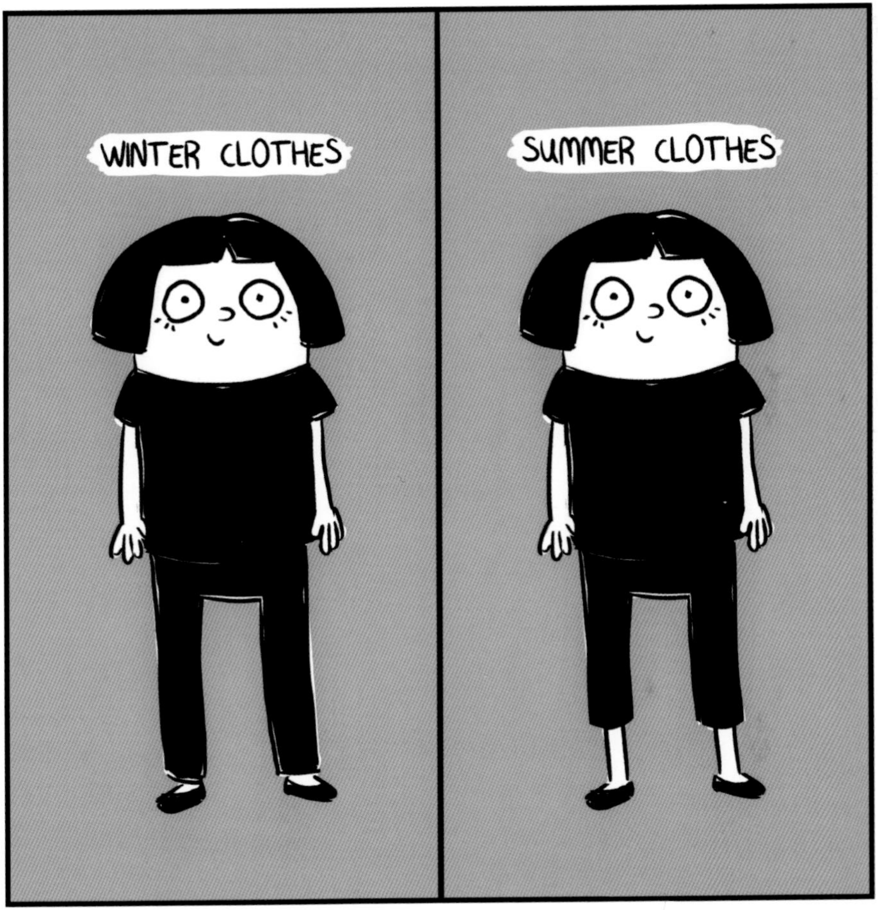
WINTER CLOTHES
SUMMER CLOTHES

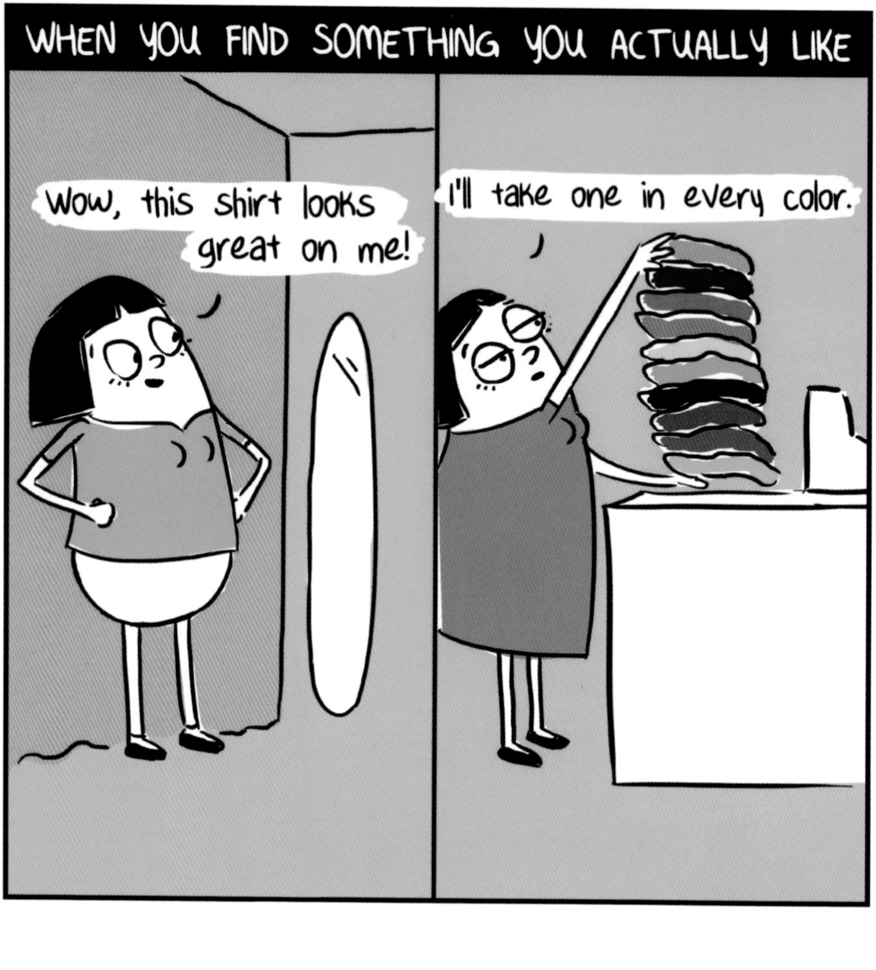
WHEN YOU FIND SOMETHING YOU ACTUALLY LIKE
Wow, this shirt looks great on me!
I'll take one in every color.

TAKE ADVANTAGE OF THE MAGIC OF MAKEUP.

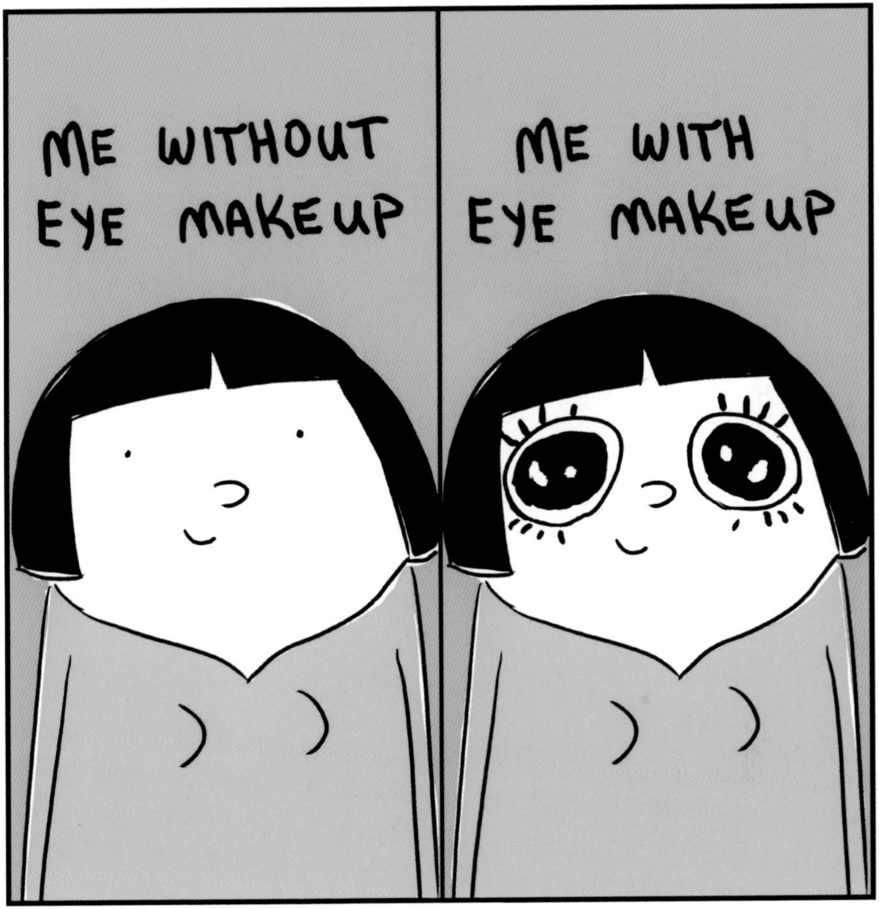
ME WITHOUT EYE MAKEUP
ME WITH EYE MAKEUP

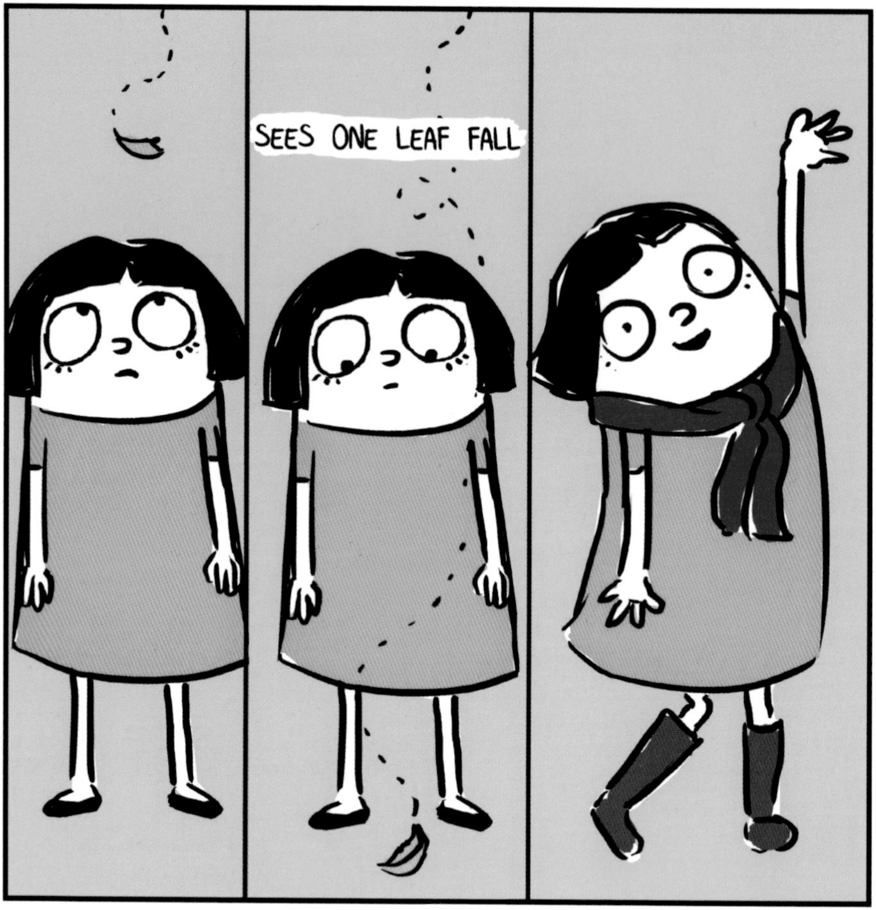
SEES ONE LEAF FALL

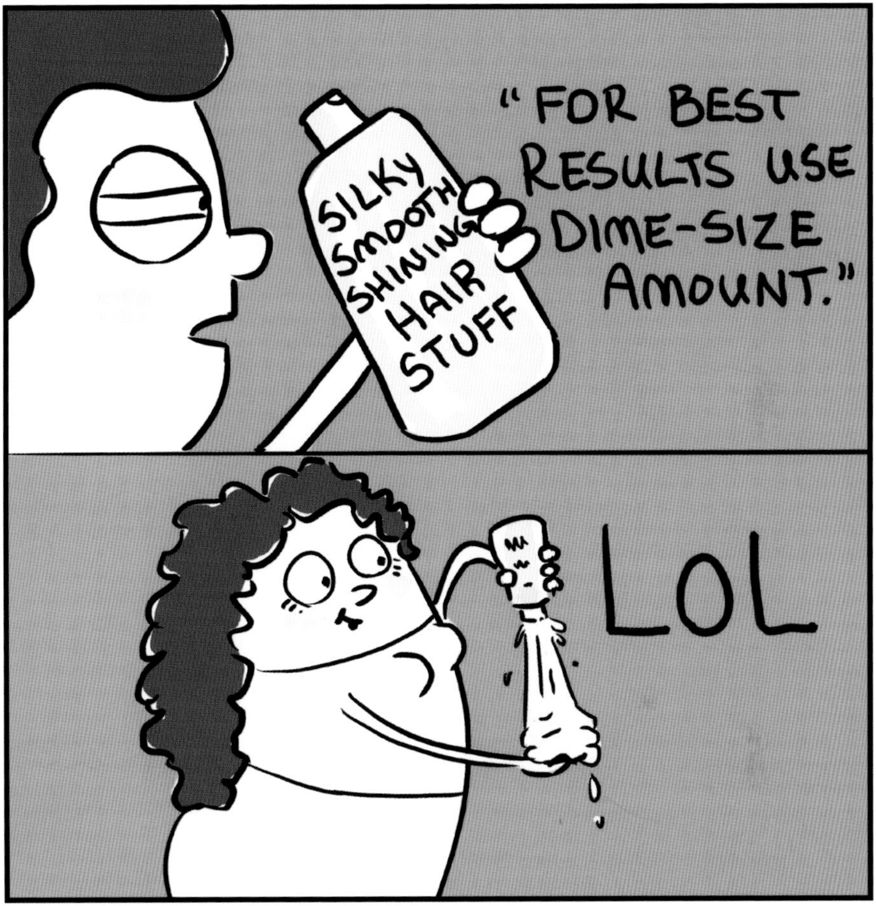
"FOR BEST RESULTS USE DIME-SIZE AMOUNT."
SILKY SMOOTH SHINING HAIR STUFF
LOL

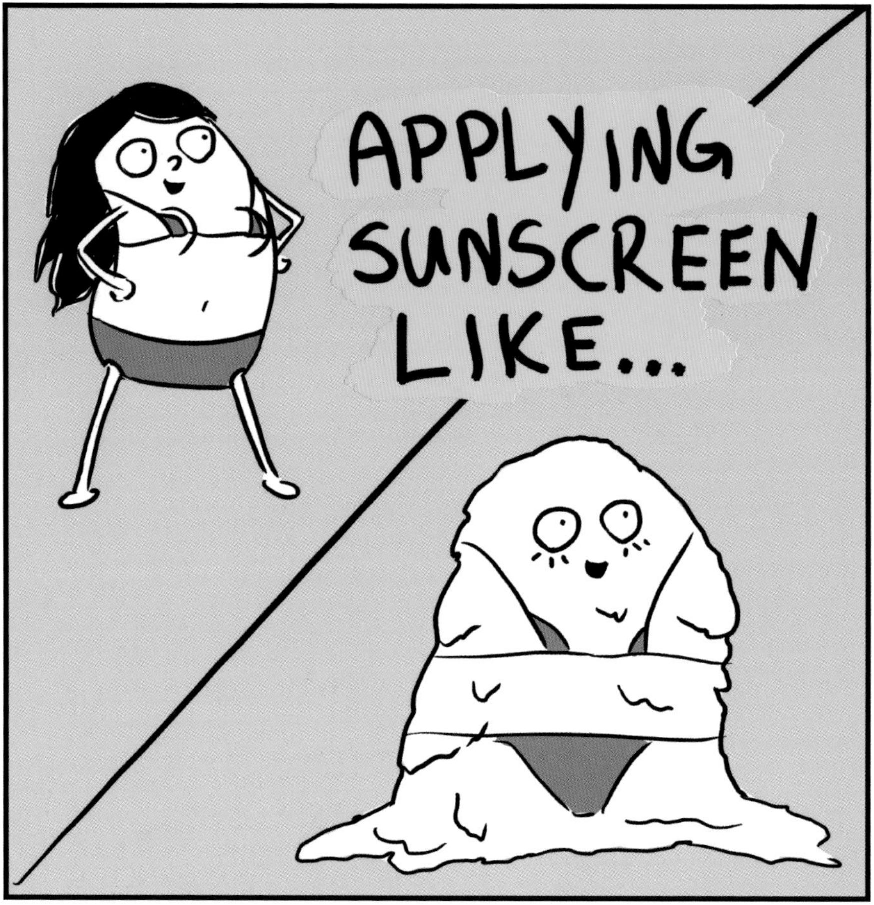
APPLYING SUNSCREEN LIKE...

SURPRISE ROMANCE MAY AWAIT IF YOU FORGET TO WASH YOUR FACE ENOUGH.

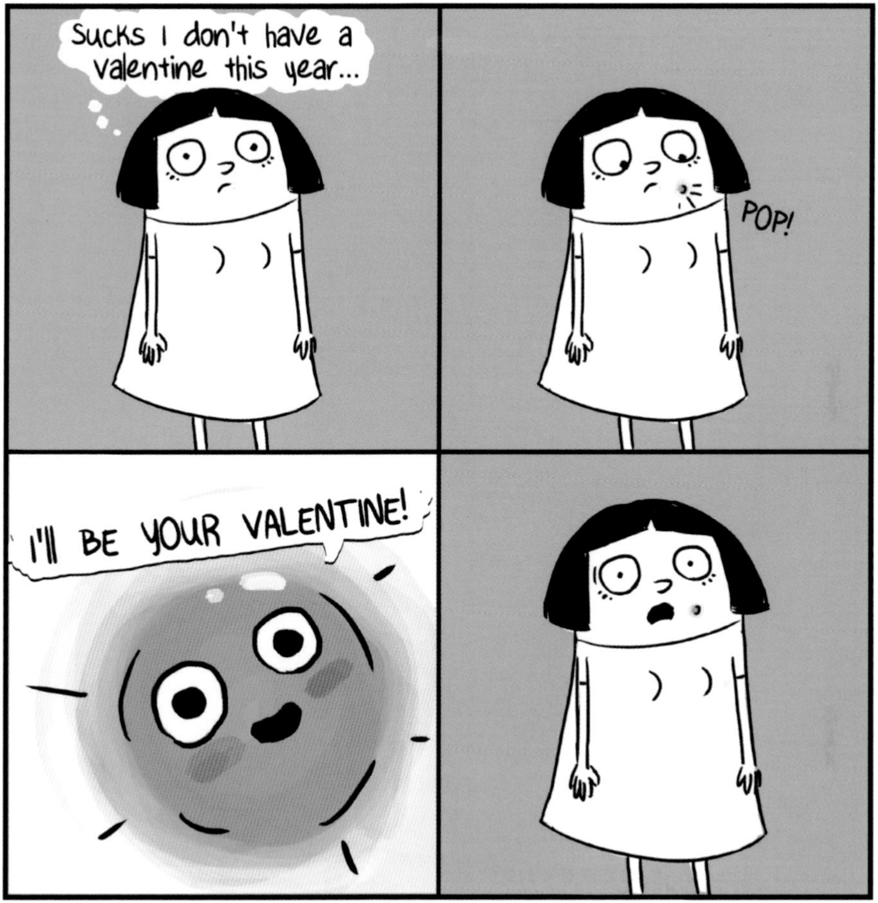
Sucks I don't have a valentine this year...
POP!
I'll BE YOUR VALENTINE!

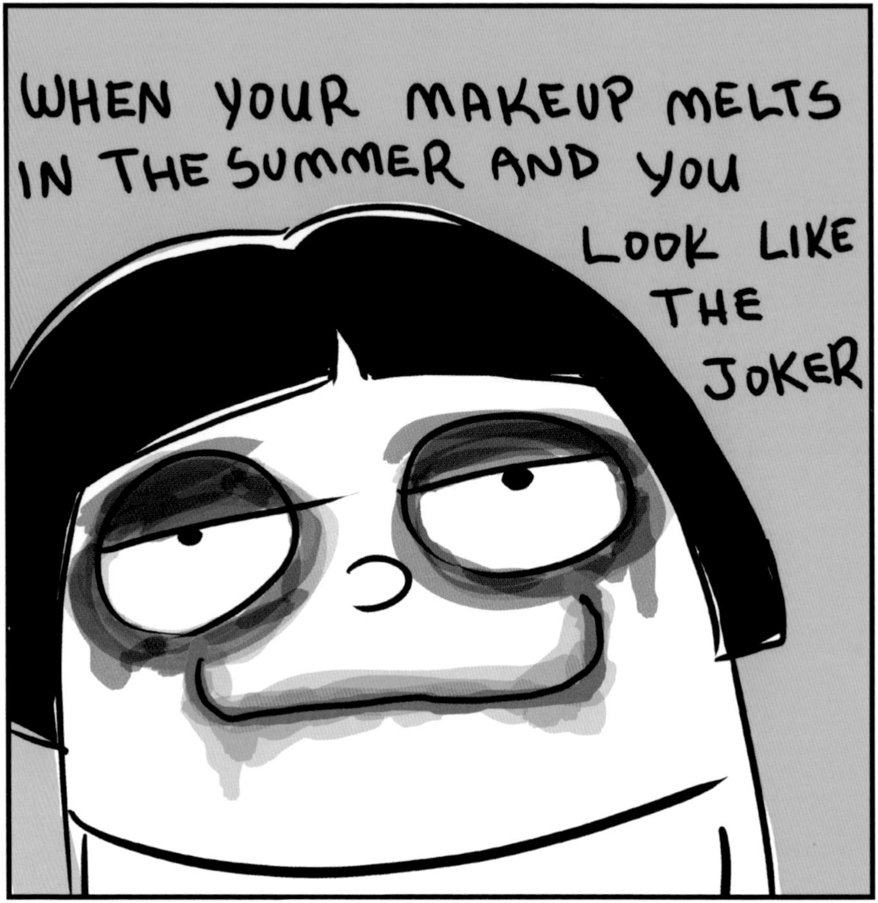
WHEN YOUR MAKEUP MELTS IN THE SUMMER AND YOU LOOK LIKE THE JOKER

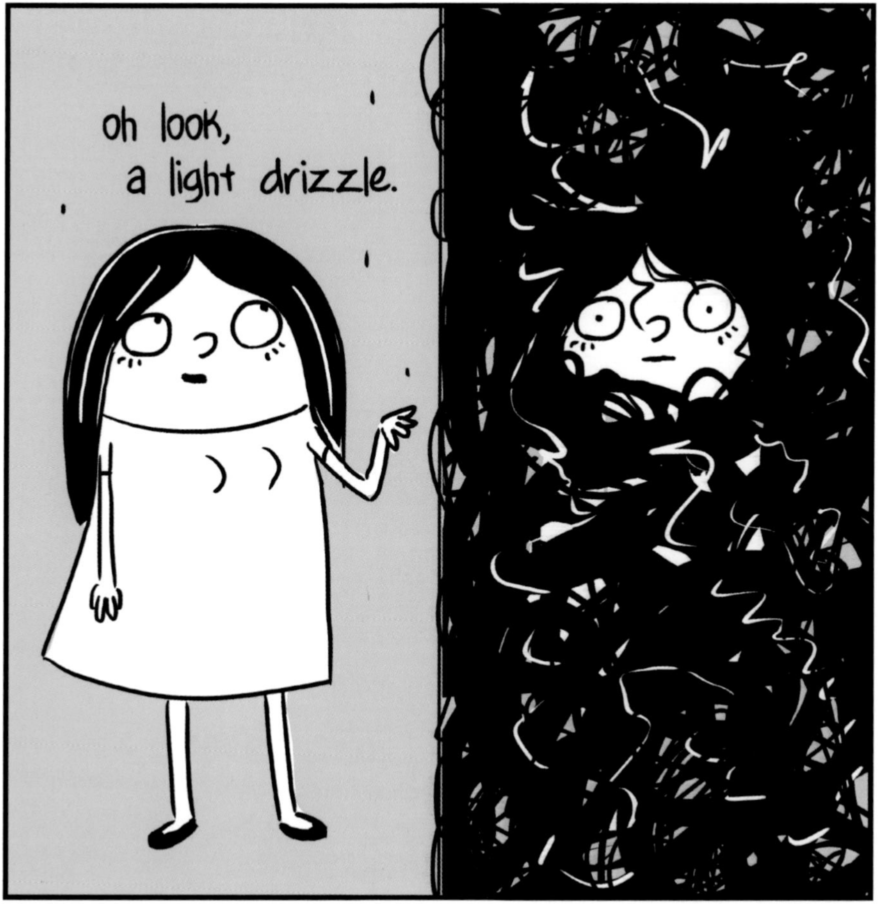
oh look,
a light drizzle.

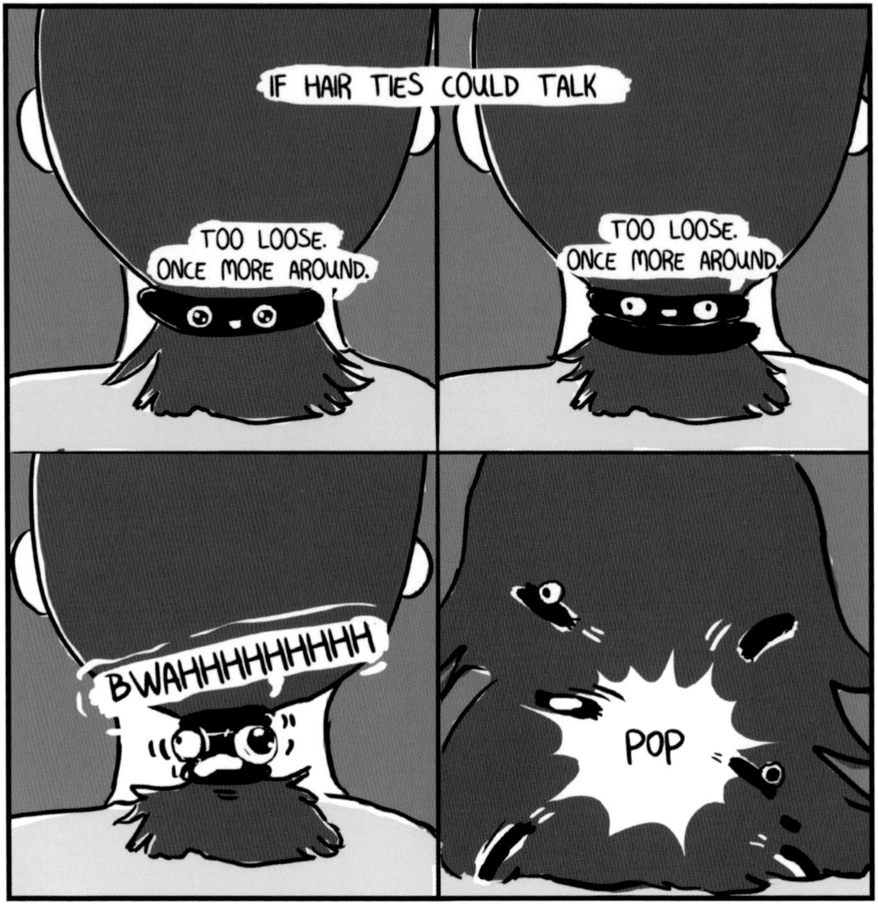
IF HAIR TIES COULD TALK
TOO LOOSE. ONCE MORE AROUND.
TOO LOOSE. ONCE MORE AROUND.
BWAHHHHHHHHH
POP

FUZZY LEGS ARE COZIER.

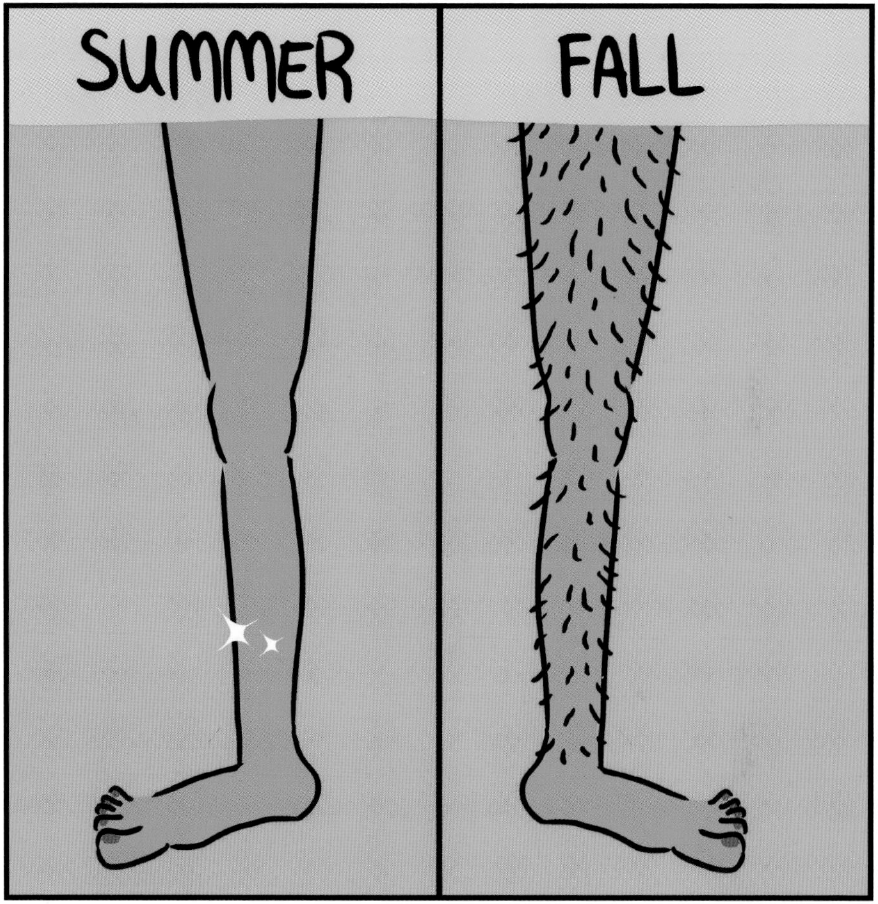
SUMMER
FALL

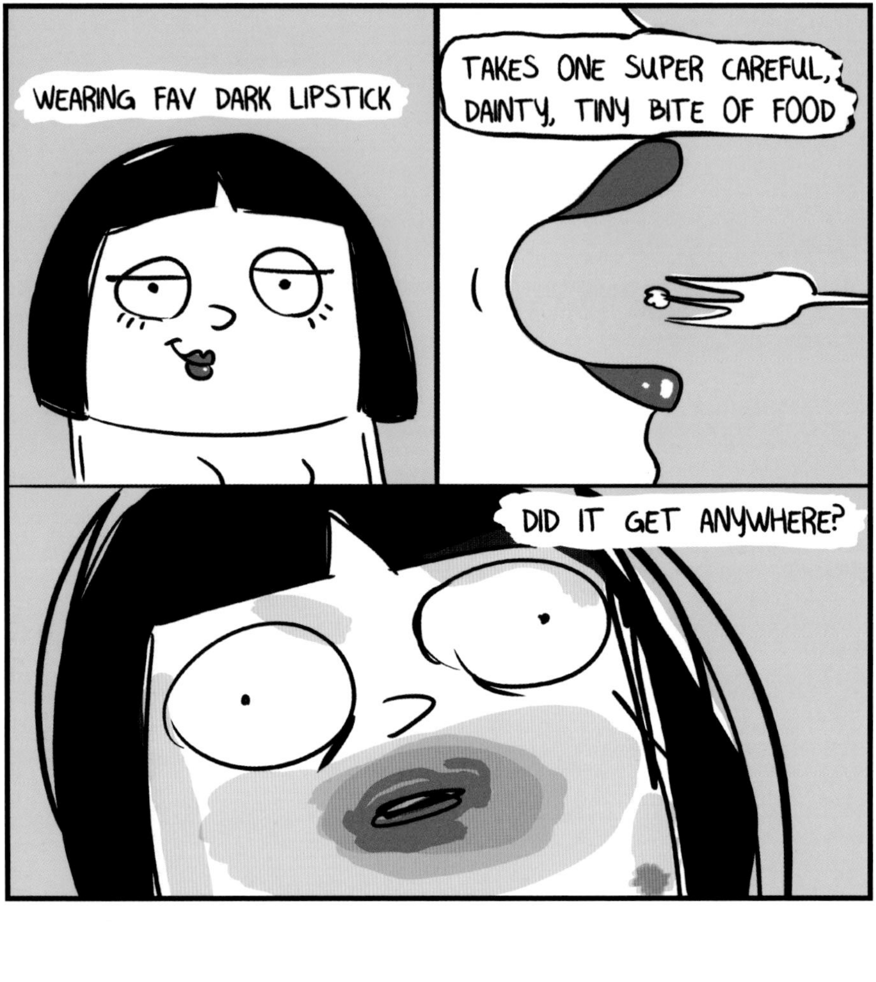
WEARING FAV DARK LIPSTICK
TAKES ONE SUPER CAREFUL, DAINTY, TINY BITE OF FOOD
DID IT GET ANYWHERE?

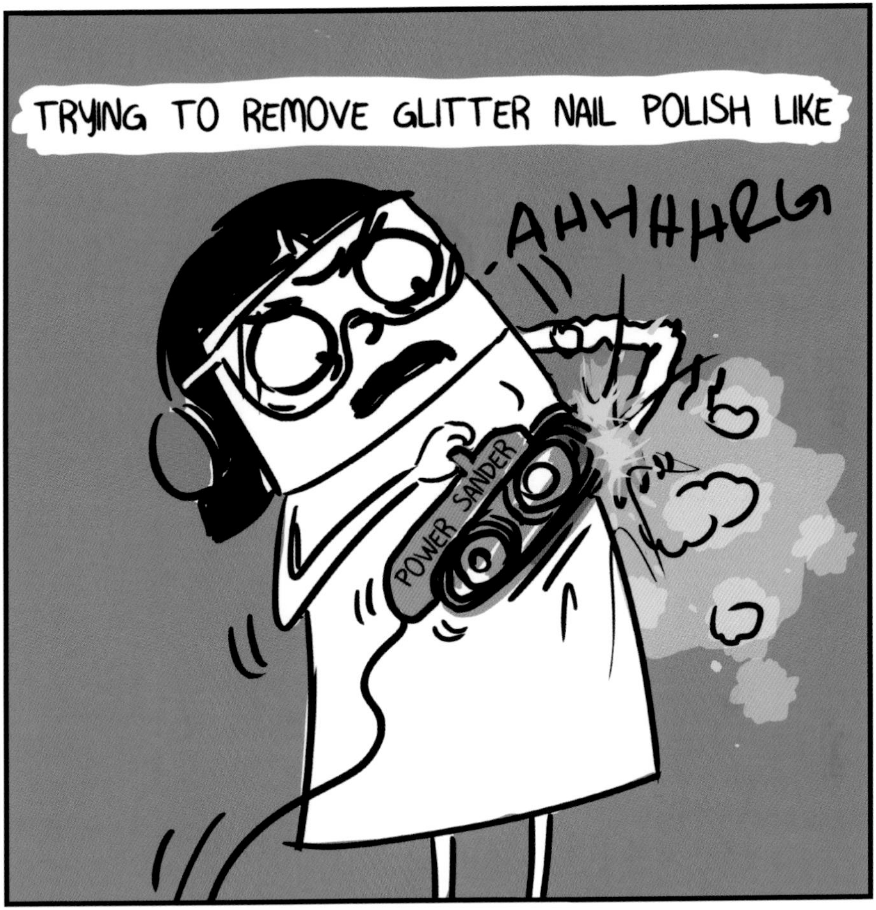
TRYING TO REMOVE GLITTER NAIL POLISH LIKE
AHHHHRG
POWER SANDER

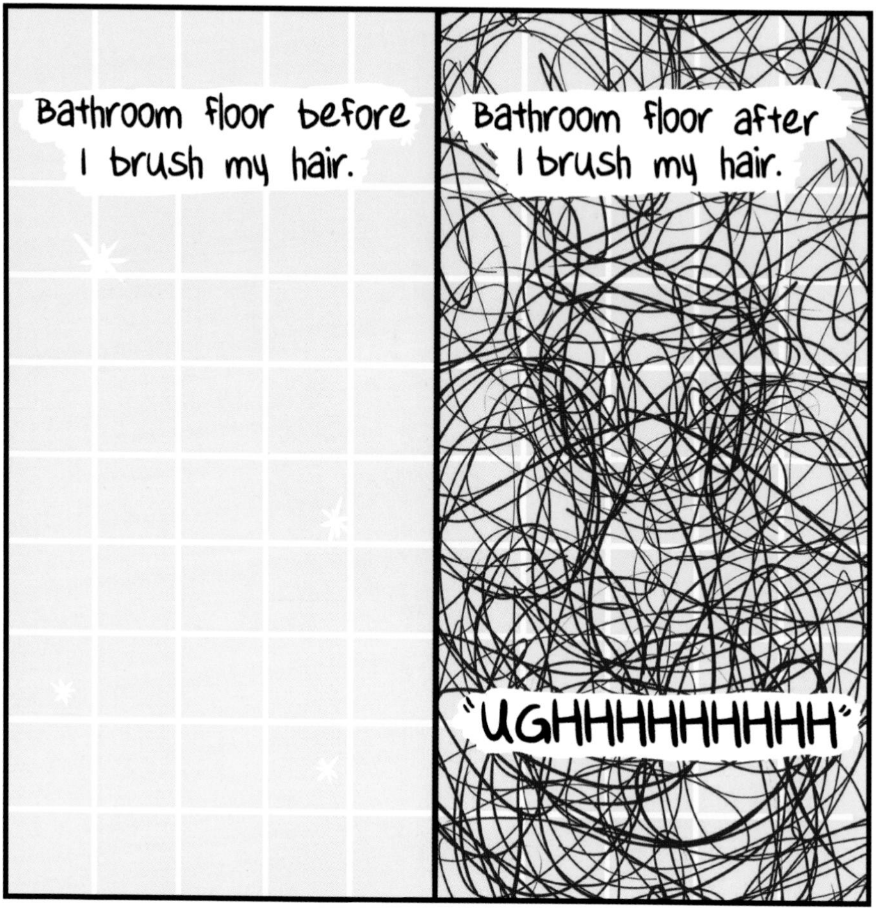
Bathroom floor before I brush my hair.
Bathroom floor after I brush my hair.
"UGHHHHHHHHH"

DON'T FORGET TO PREPARE IN ADVANCE FOR YOUR FASHION DECISIONS.

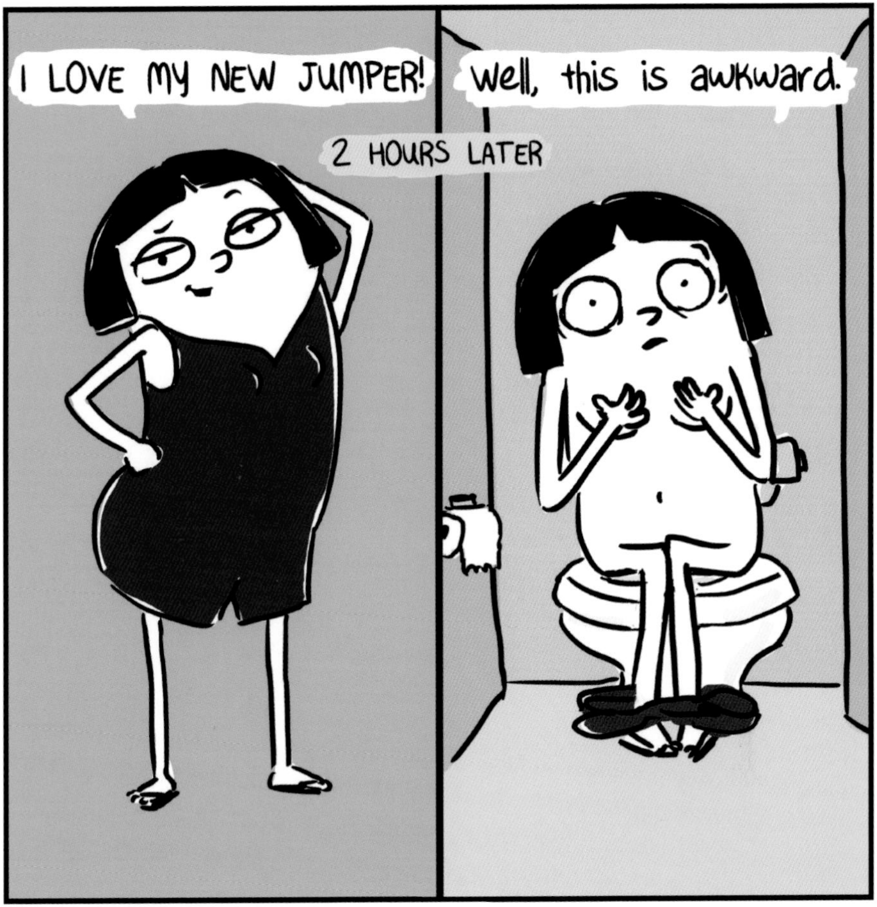
I LOVE MY NEW JUMPER!
2 HOURS LATER
Well, this is awkward.

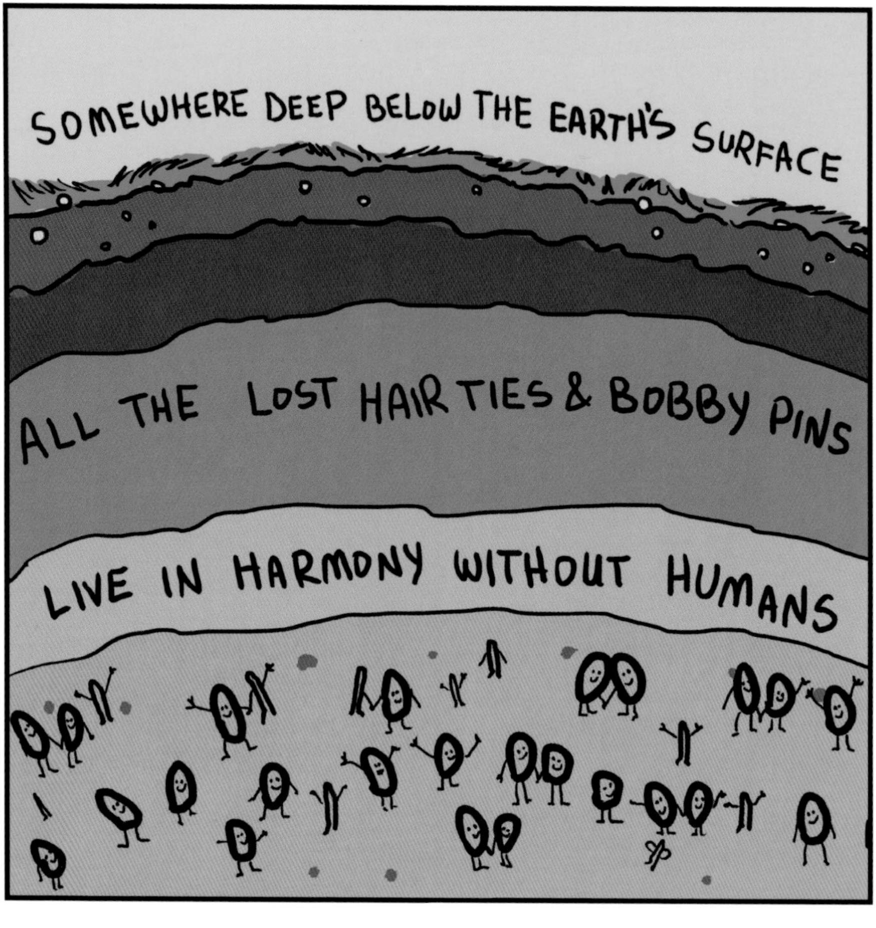
SOMEWHERE DEEP BELOW THE EARTH'S SURFACE
ALL THE LOST HAIR TIES & BOBBY PINS
LIVE IN HARMONY WITHOUT HUMANS

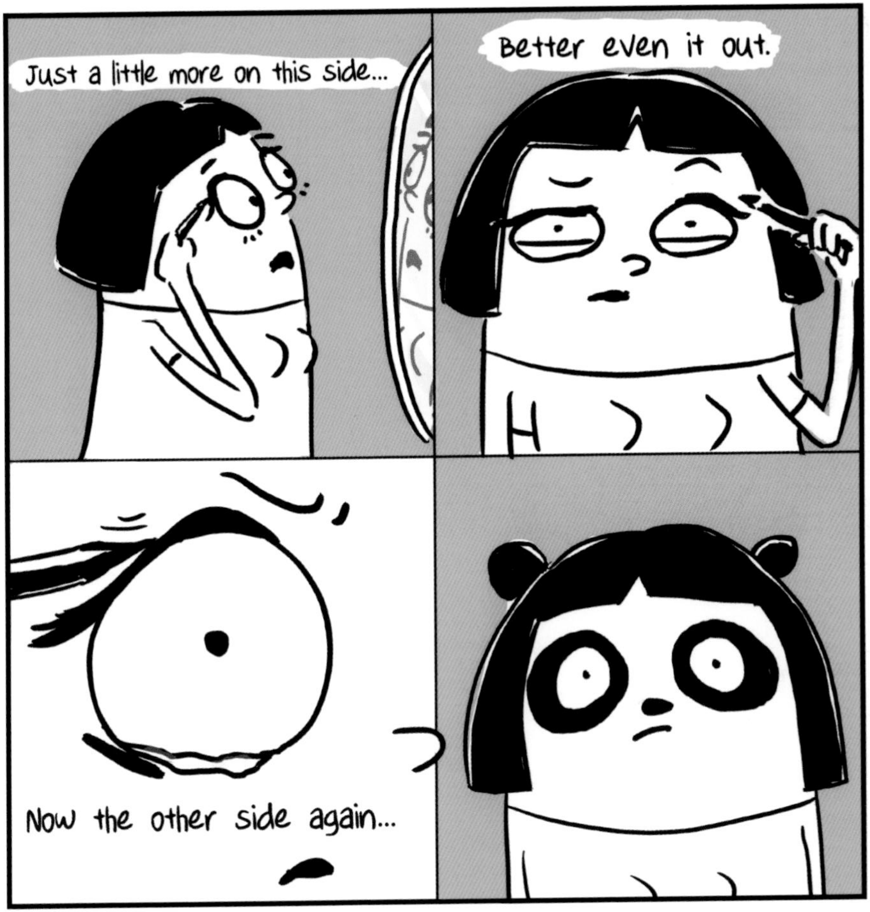
Just a little more on this side...
Better even it out.
Now the other side again...

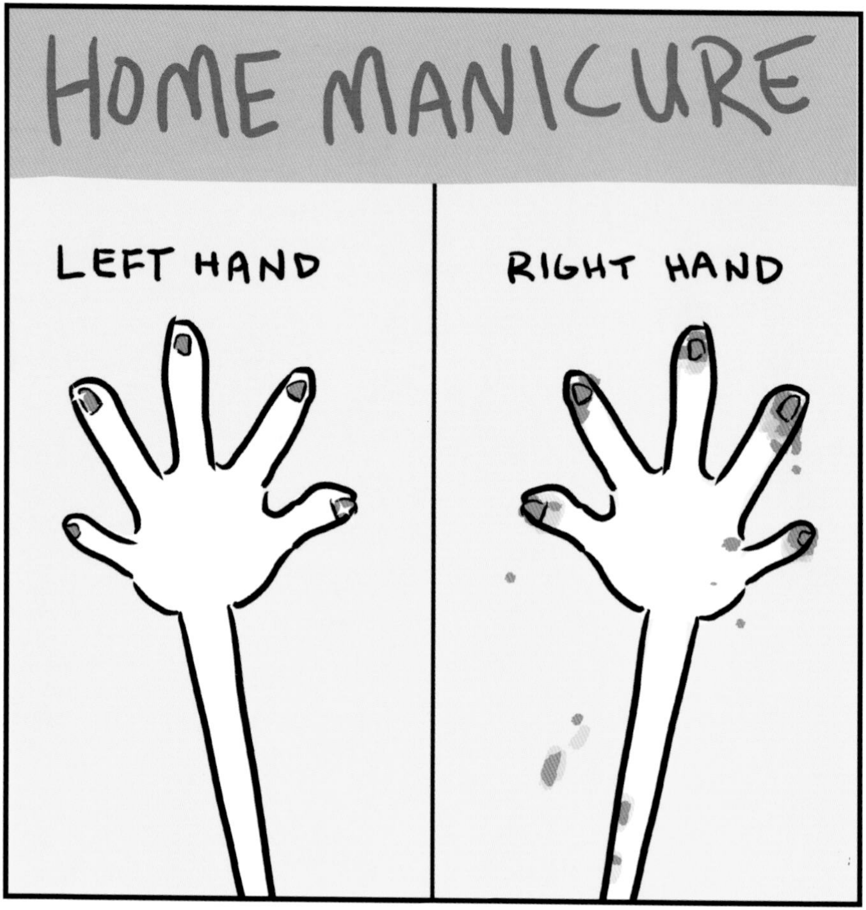
HOME MANICURE
LEFT HAND
RIGHT HAND

A MANICURE IS ONLY AS AWKWARD AS YOU MAKE IT.

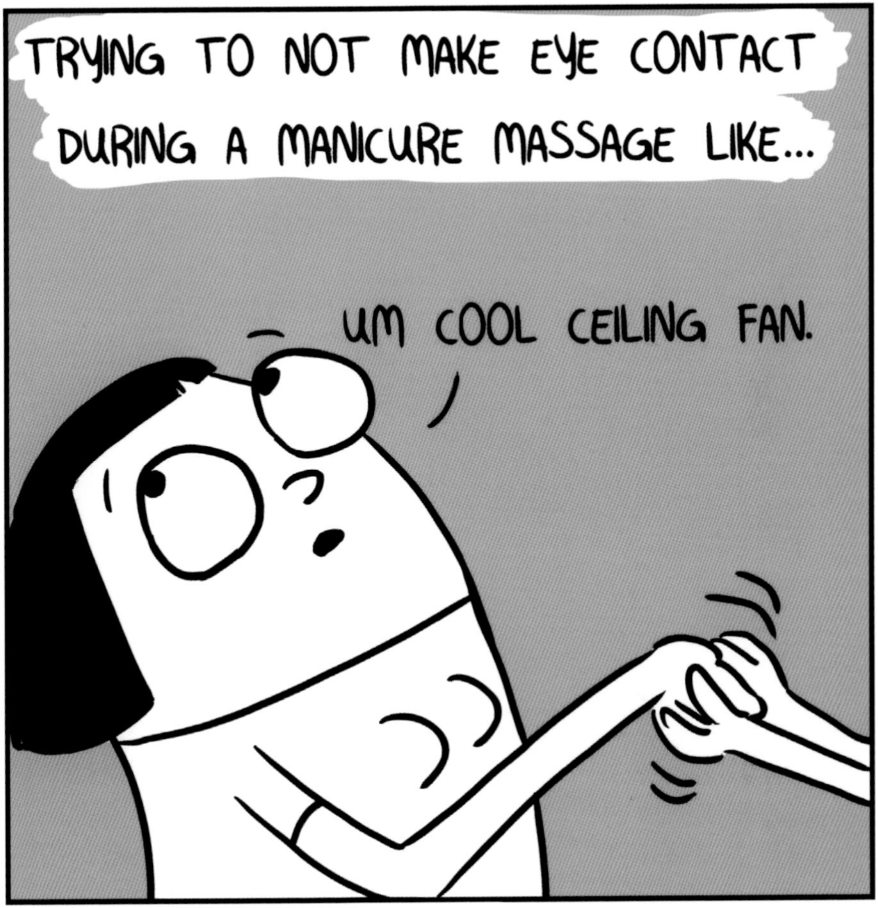
TRYING TO NOT MAKE EYE CONTACT DURING A MANICURE MASSAGE LIKE...
UM COOL CEILING FAN.

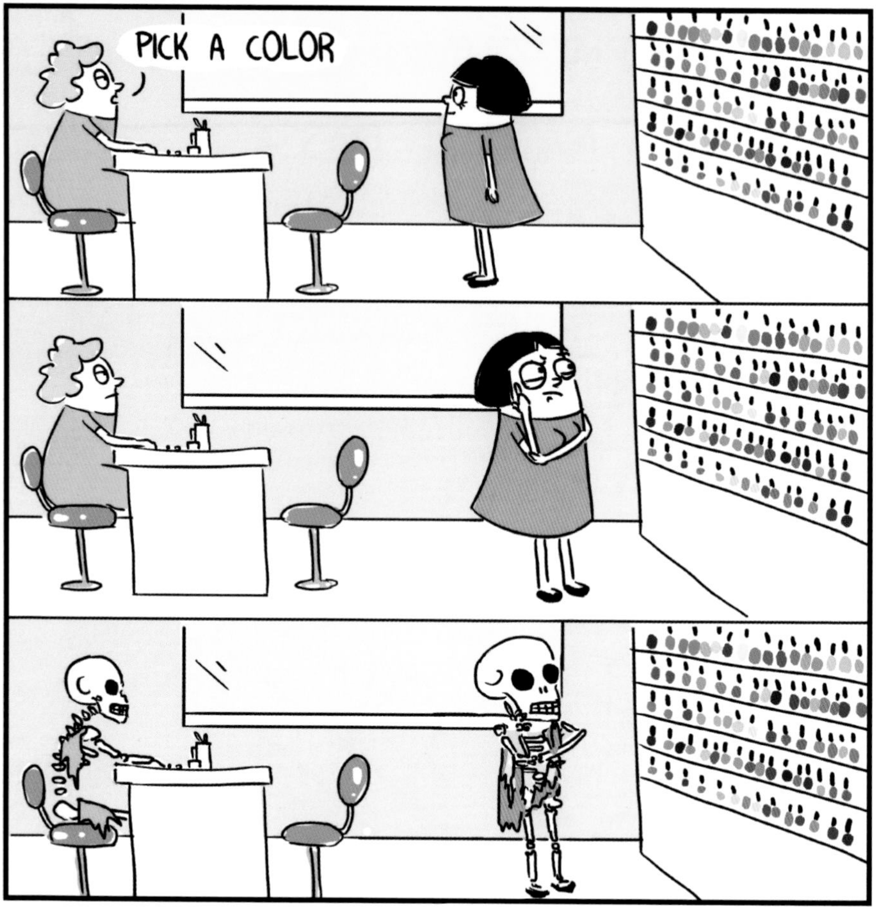
PICK A COLOR

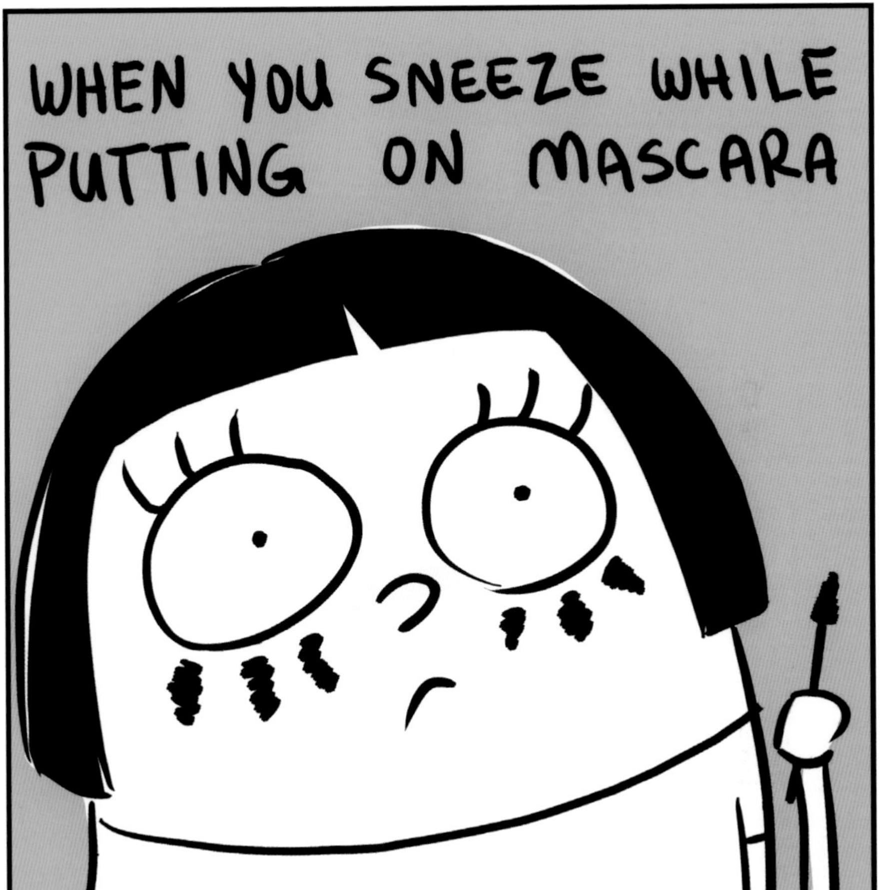
WHEN YOU SNEEZE WHILE PUTTING ON MASCARA

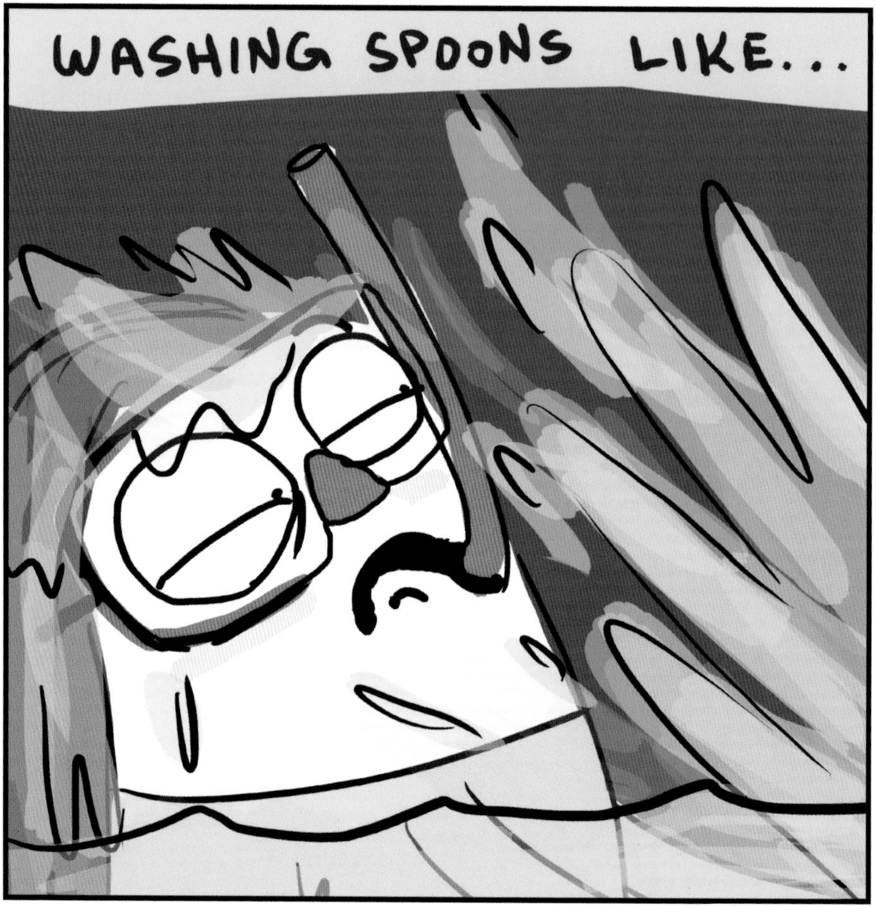
WASHING SPOONS LIKE...

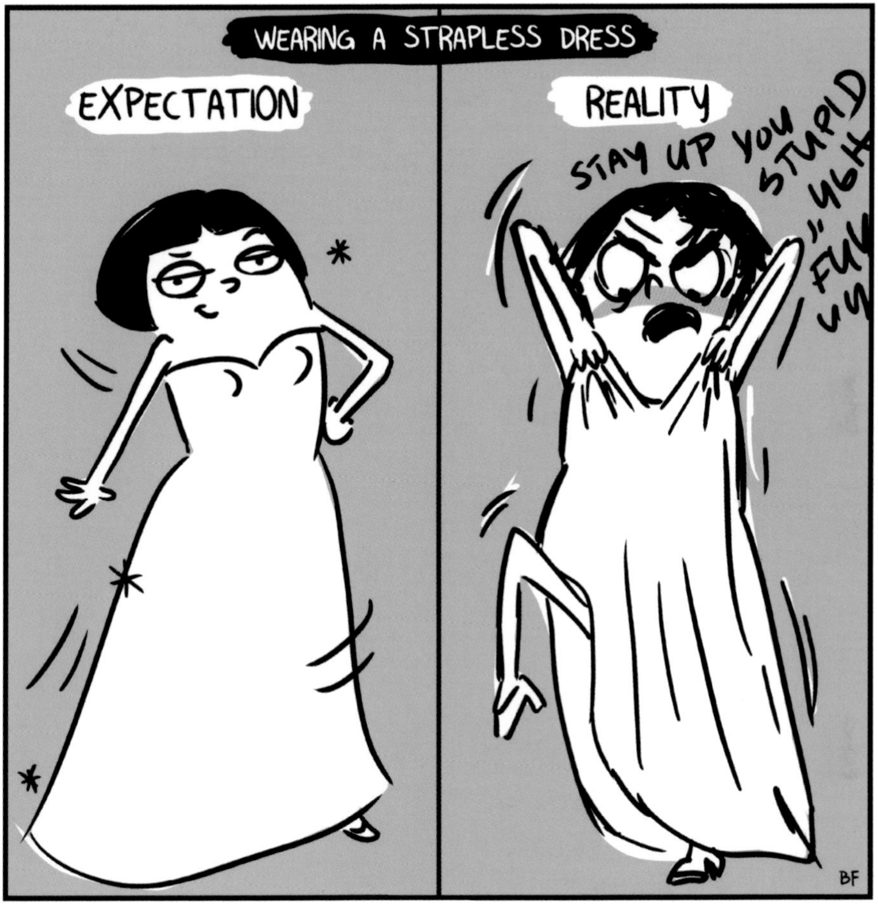
WEARING A STRAPLESS DRESS
EXPECTATION
REALITY
STAY UP YOU STUPID UGH
BF

EMBRACE THE CHAOS.

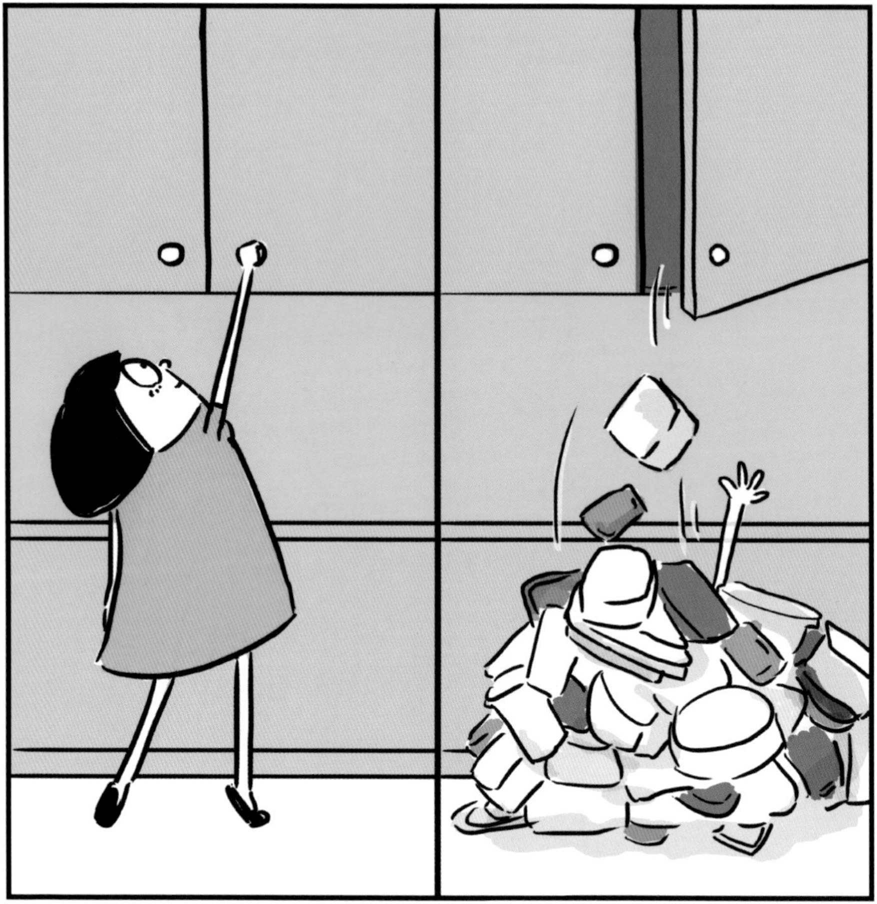

LIFE
AMBITIONS

STOP AND SEE THE BEAUTY IN EVERYTHING.

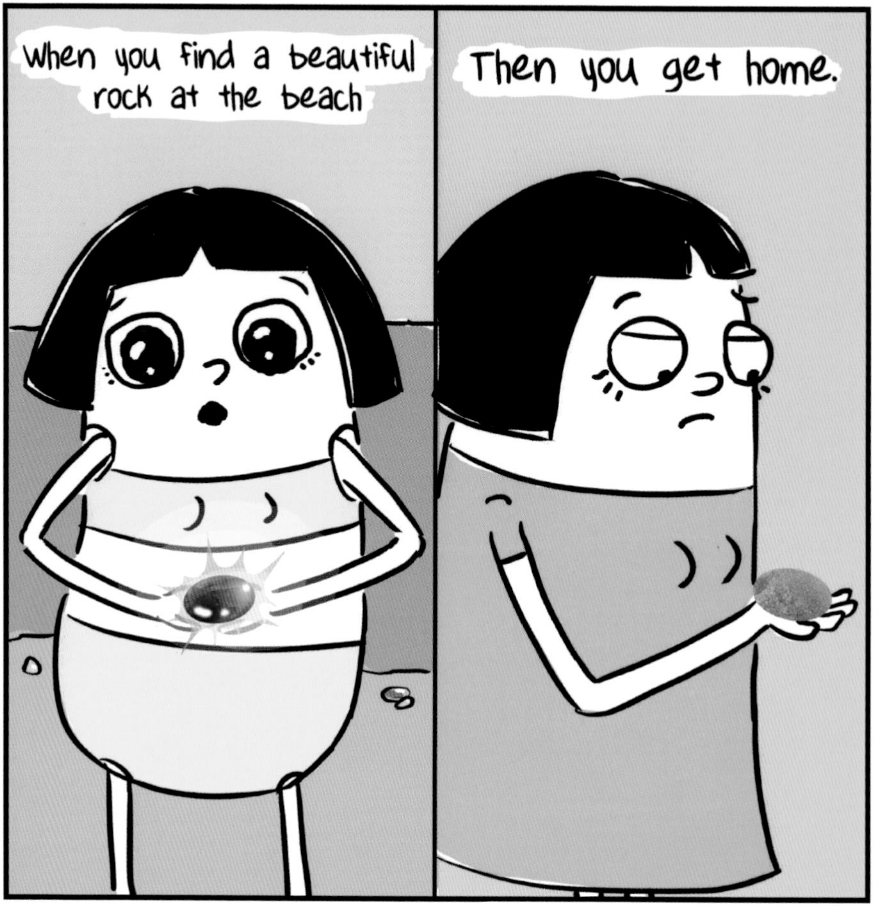
When you find a beautiful rock at the beach
Then you get home.

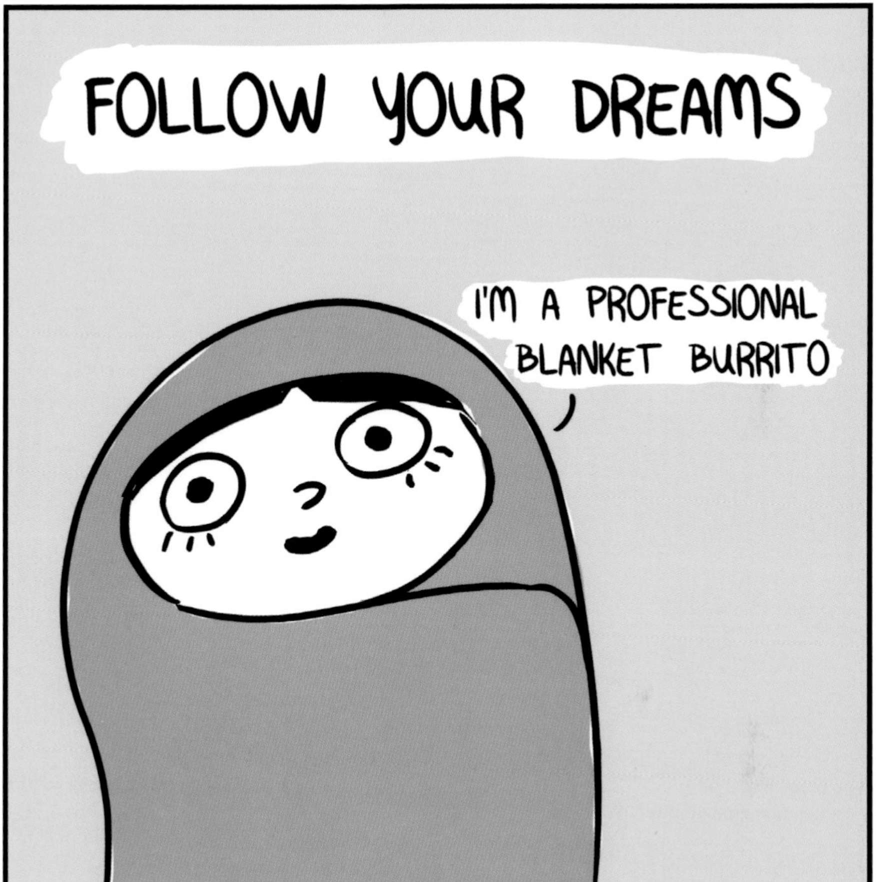
FOLLOW YOUR DREAMS
I'M A PROFESSIONAL BLANKET BURRITO

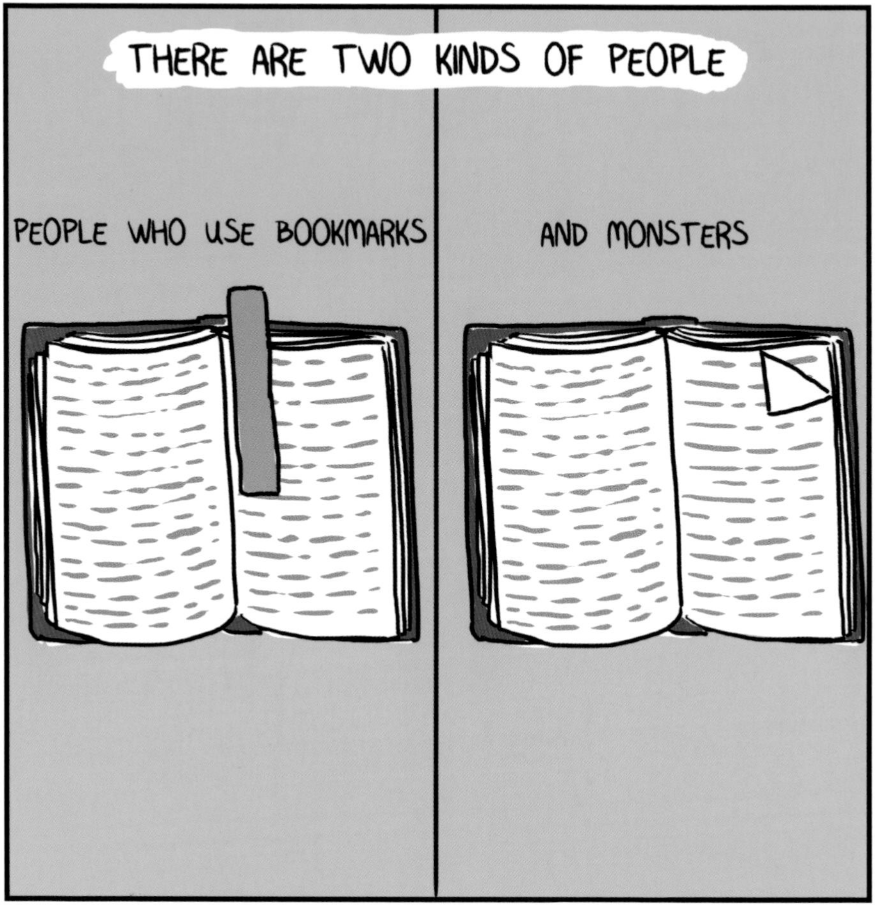
THERE ARE TWO KINDS OF PEOPLE
PEOPLE WHO USE BOOKMARKS
AND MONSTERS

DON'T OVERTHINK THINGS.

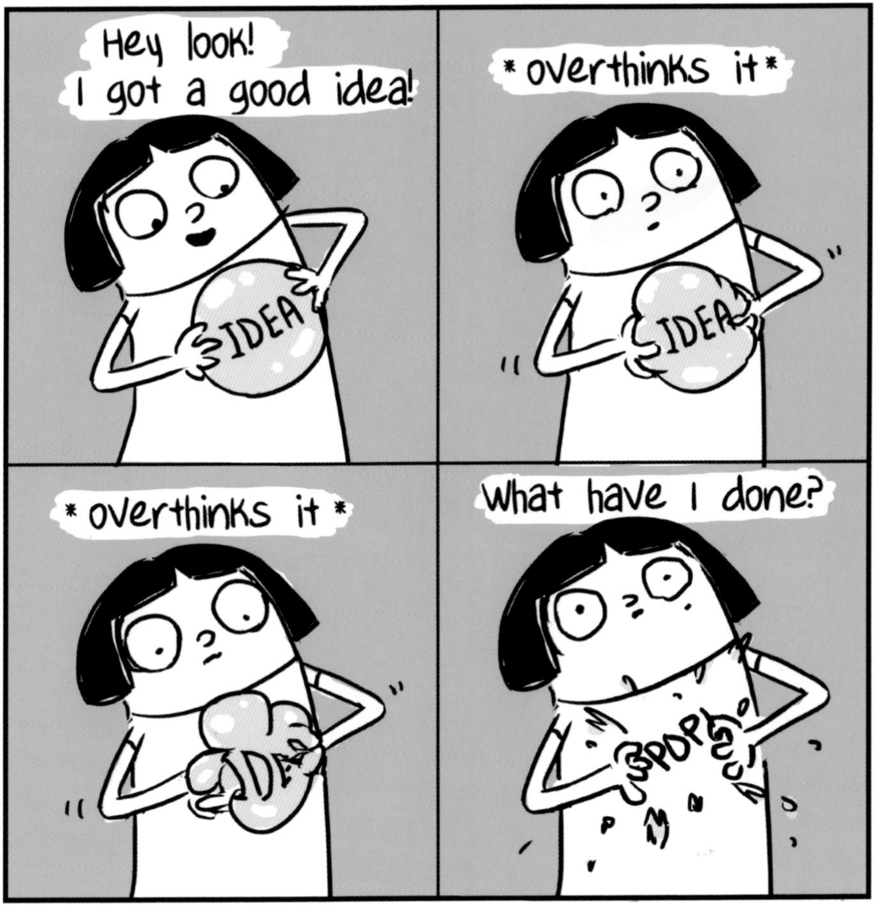
Hey look!
I got a good idea!
IDEA
overthinks it
IDEA
overthinks it
What have I done?
POP

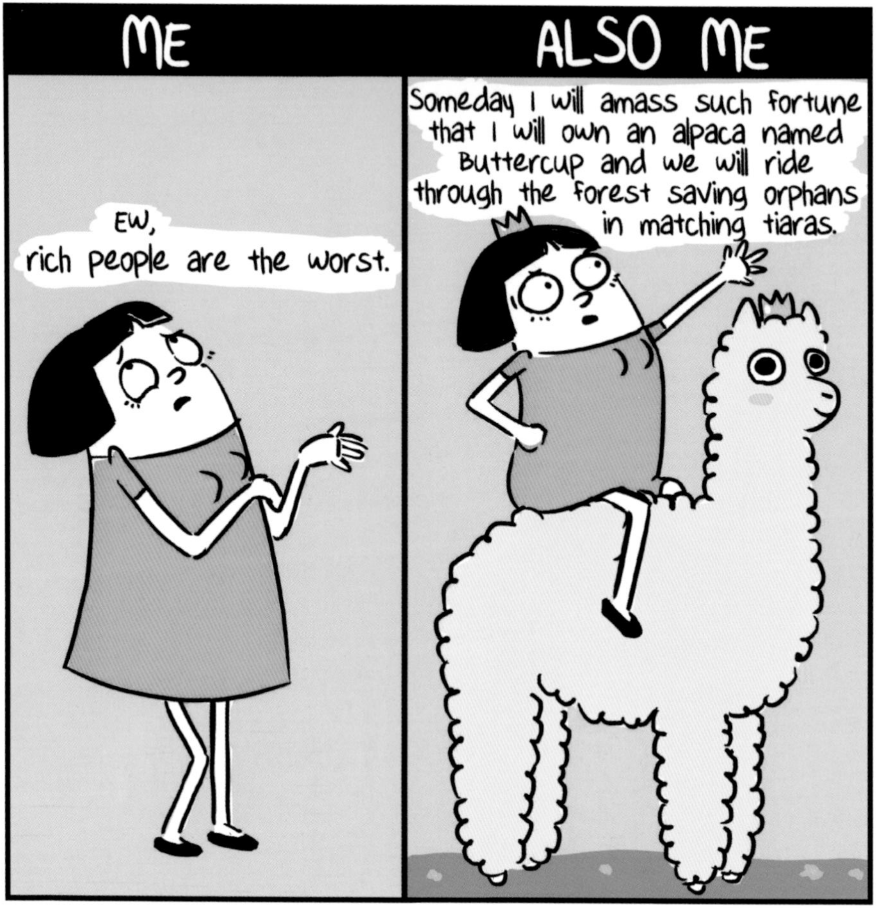
ME
ALSO ME
EW,
rich people are the worst.
Someday I will amass such fortune that I will own an alpaca named Buttercup and we will ride through the forest saving orphans in matching tiaras.

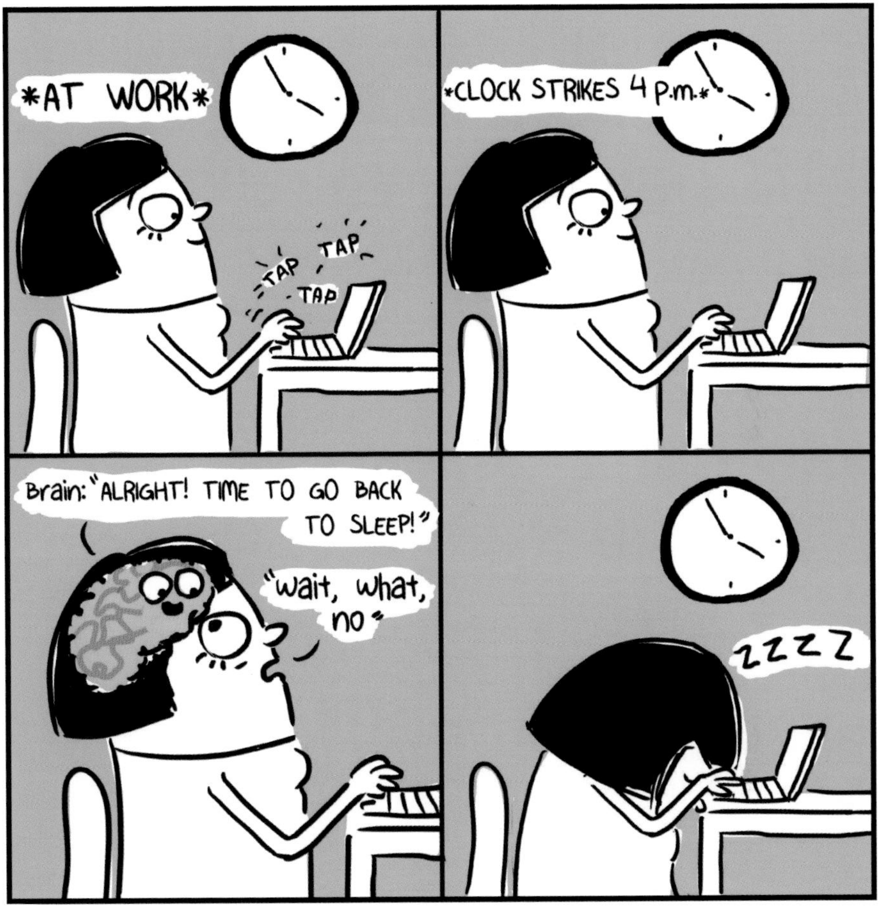
AT WORK
TAP
TAP
TAP
CLOCK STRIKES 4 p.m.
Brain: "ALRIGHT! TIME TO GO BACK TO SLEEP!"
"wait, what, no"
ZZZZ

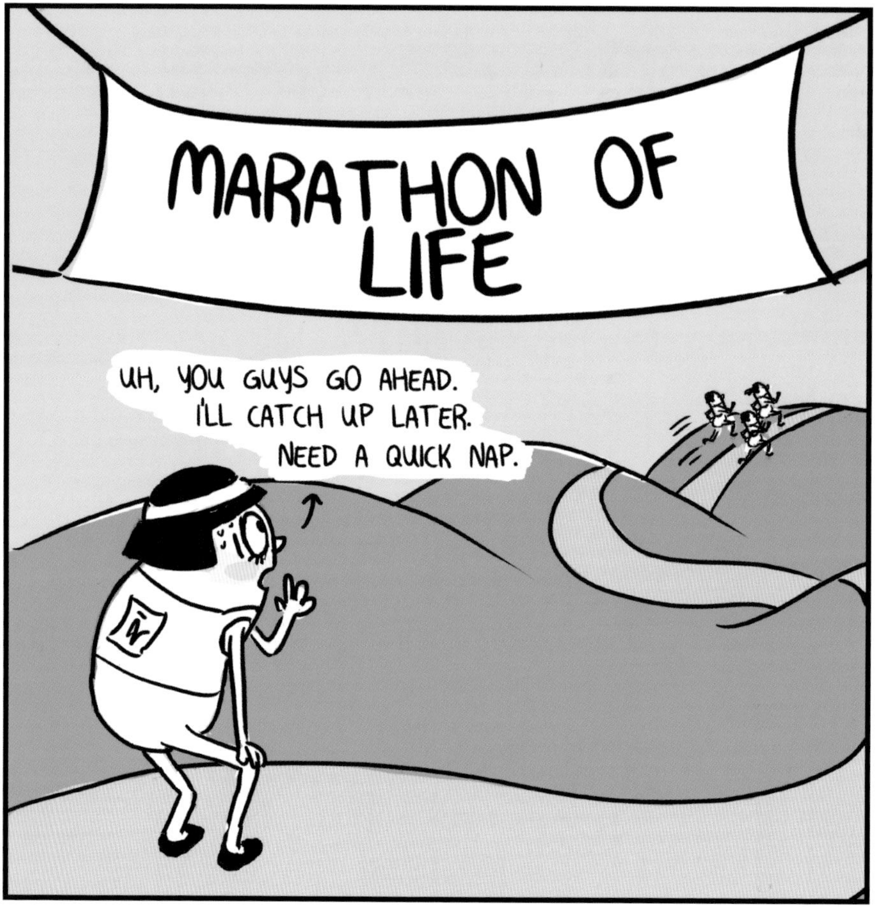
MARATHON OF LIFE
UH, YOU GUYS GO AHEAD. I'LL CATCH UP LATER. NEED A QUICK NAP.

DRESS FOR SUCCESS IN YOUR FIELD OF CHOICE.

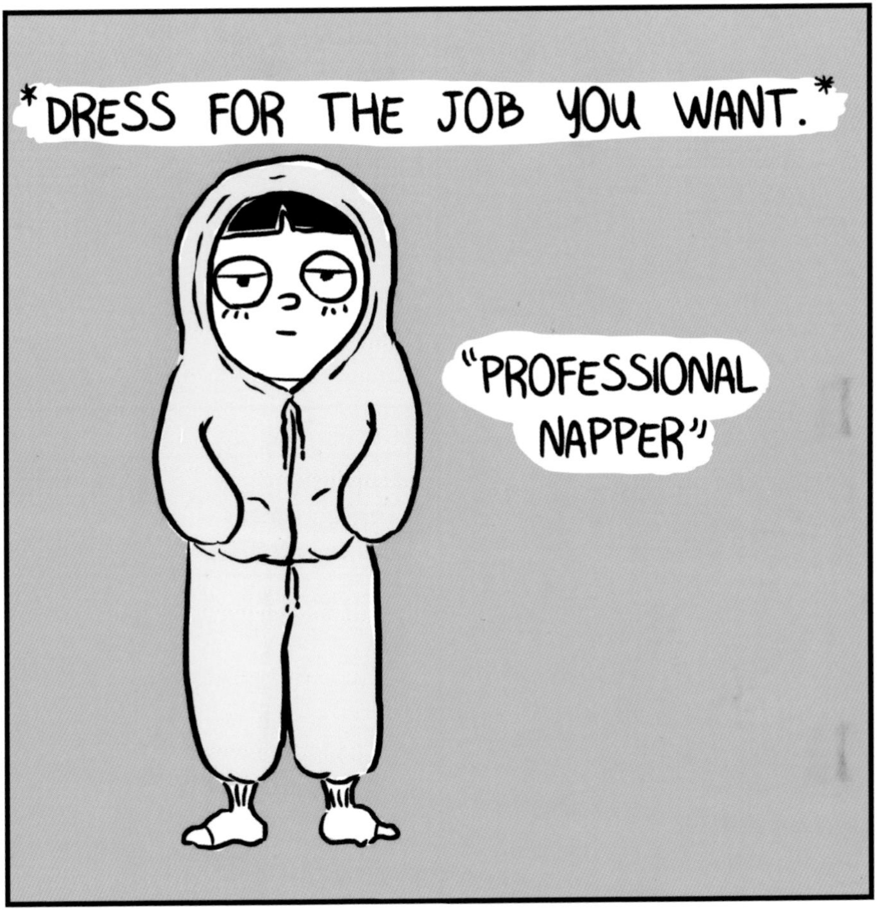
DRESS FOR THE JOB YOU WANT.
"PROFESSIONAL NAPPER"

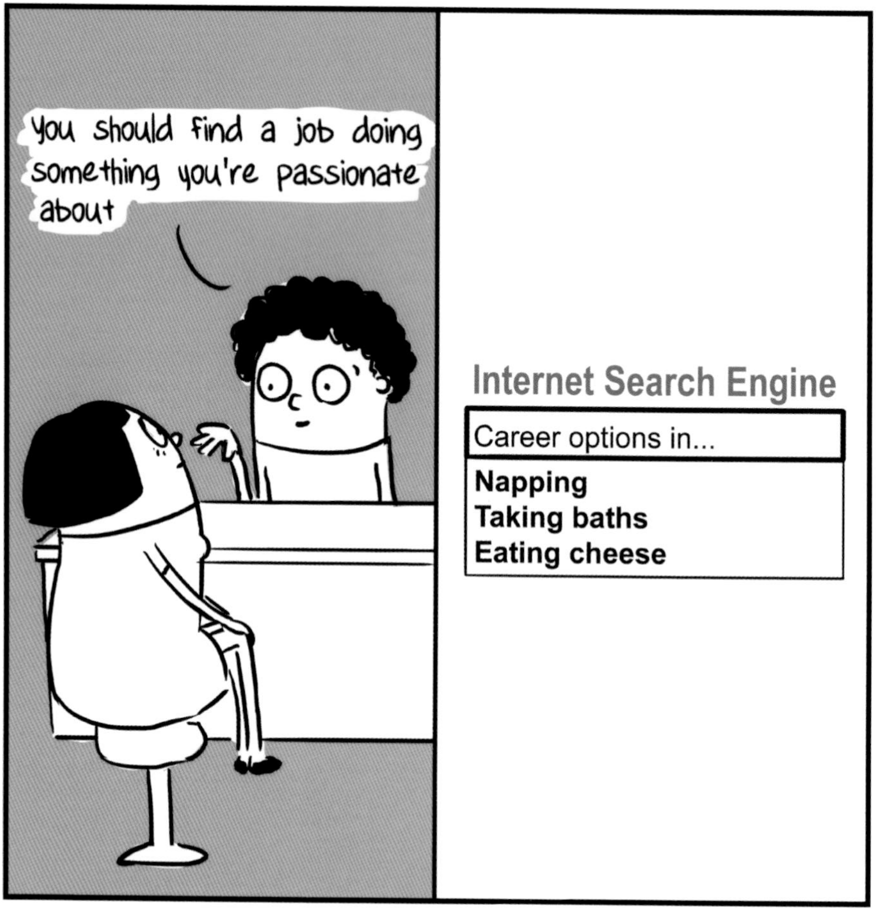
you should find a job doing something you're passionate about
Internet Search Engine
Career options in...
Napping
Taking baths
Eating cheese

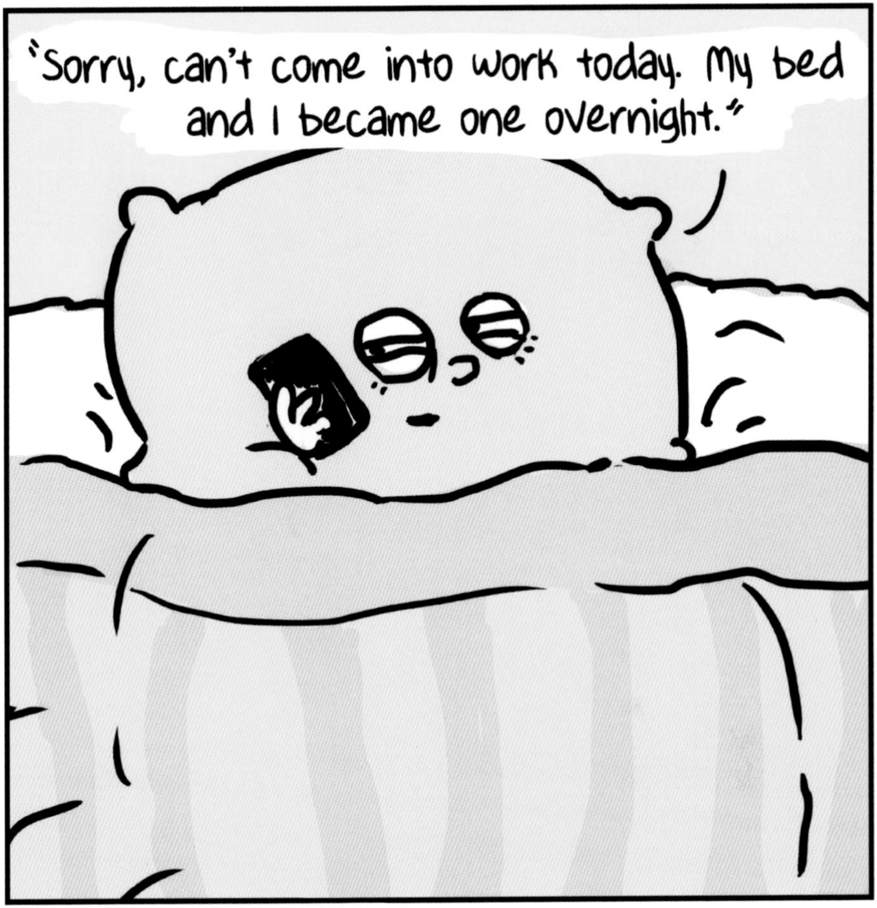
"Sorry, can't come into work today. My bed and I became one overnight."

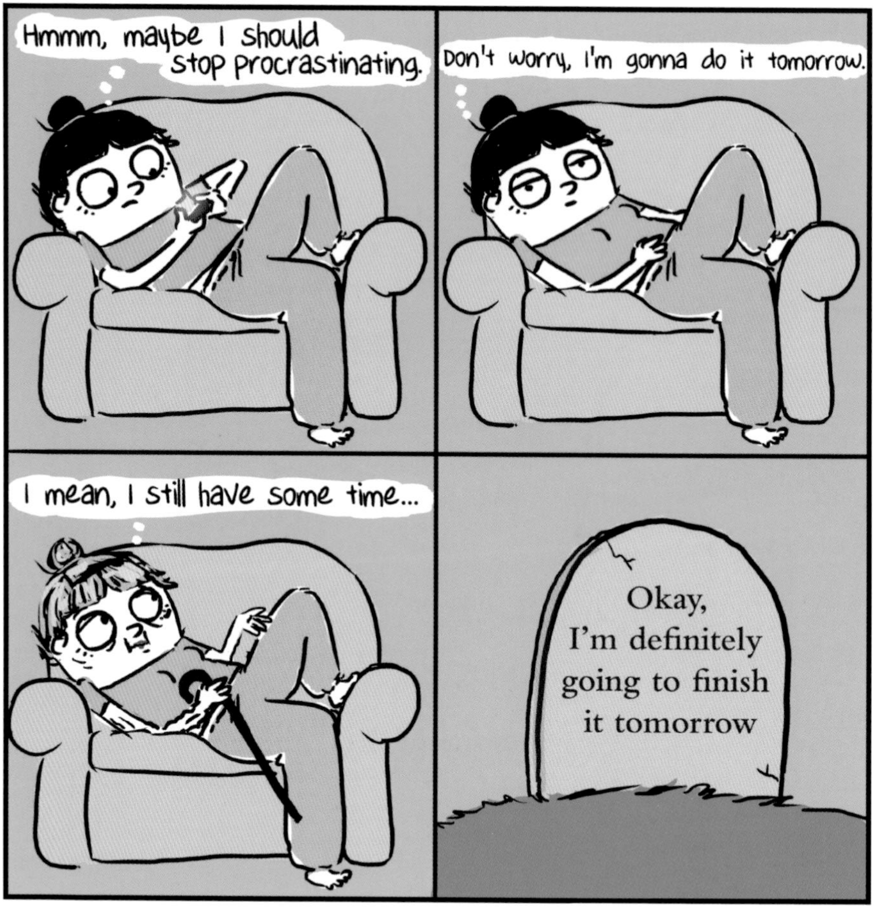
Hmmm, maybe I should stop procrastinating.
Don't worry, I'm gonna do it tomorrow.
I mean, I still have some time...
Okay,
I'm definitely
going to finish
it tomorrow

FAMILY PLANNING IS VERY IMPORTANT.

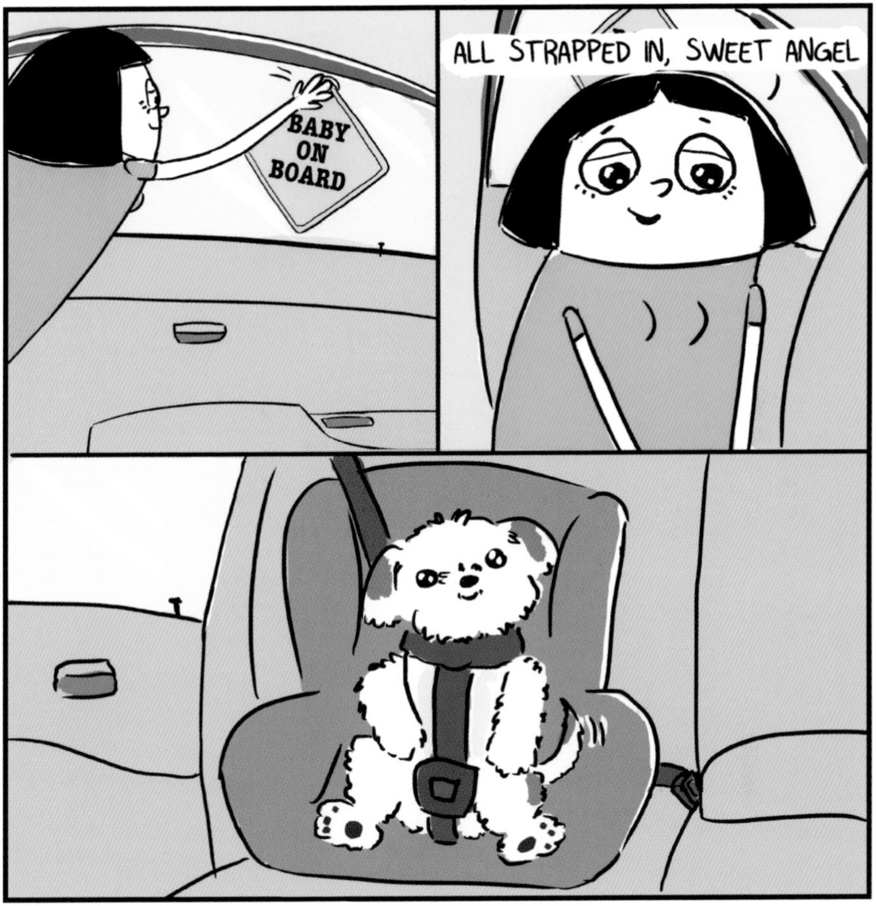

BABY ON BOARD
ALL STRAPPED IN, SWEET ANGEL

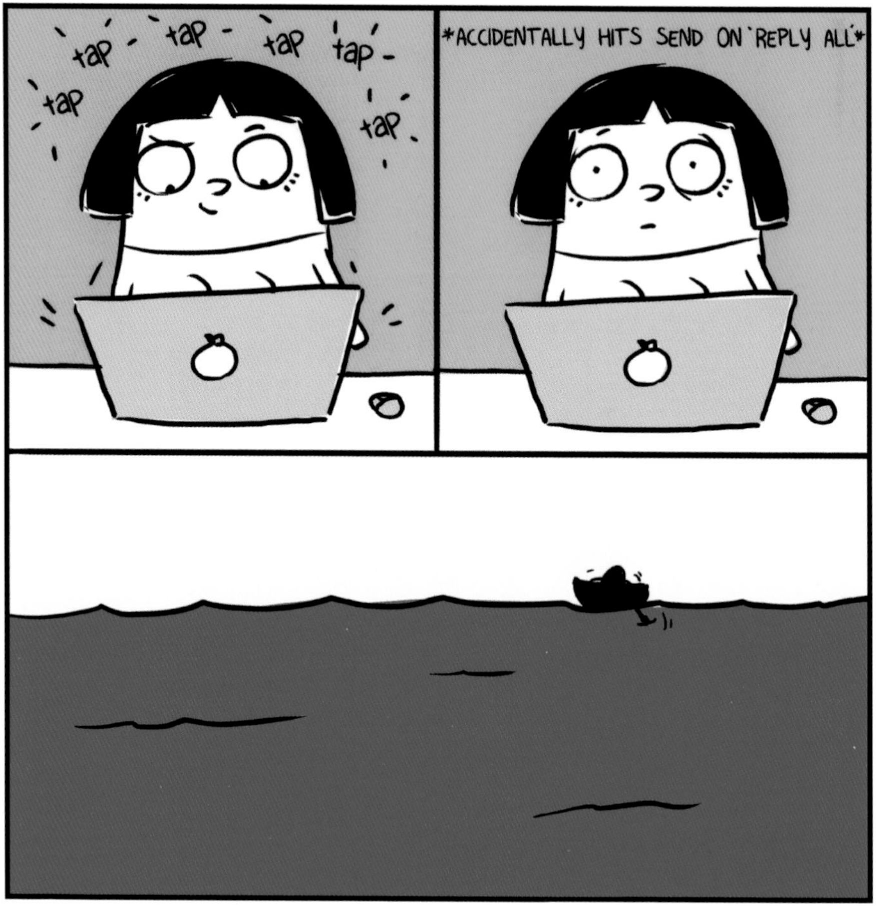
tap tap tap tap
tap tap
ACCIDENTALLY HITS SEND ON 'REPLY ALL'

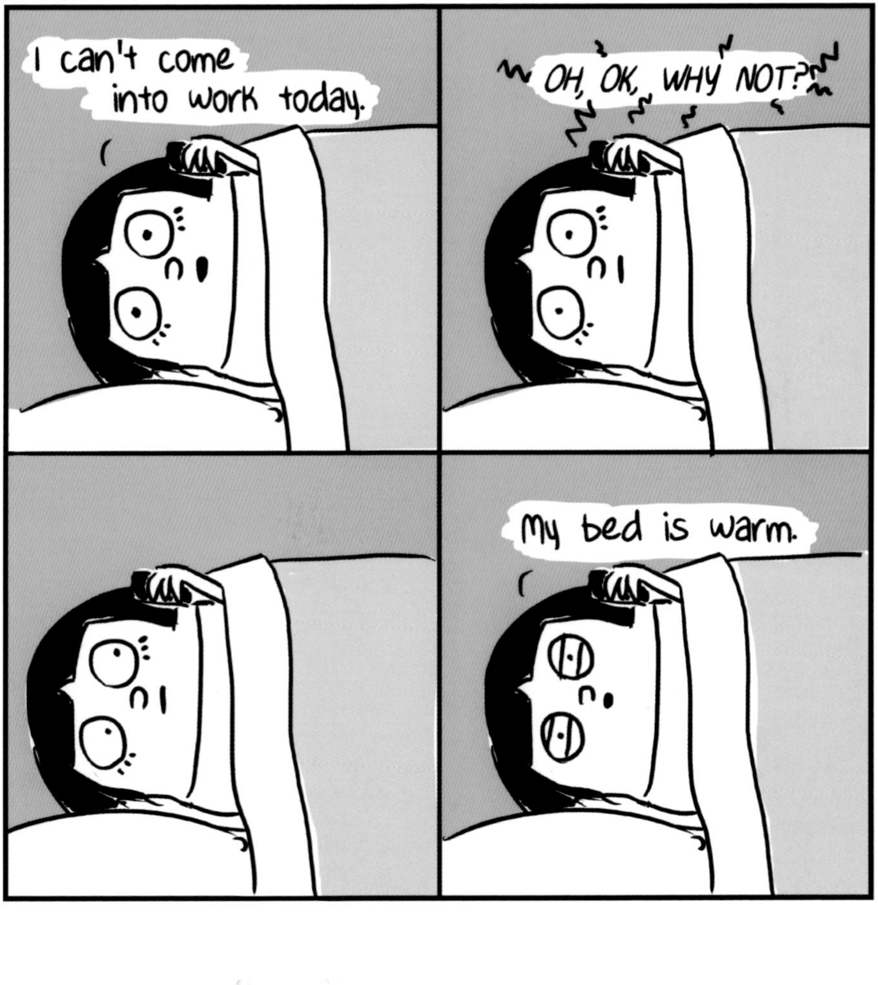
I can't come into work today.
OH, OK, WHY NOT?!
My bed is warm.

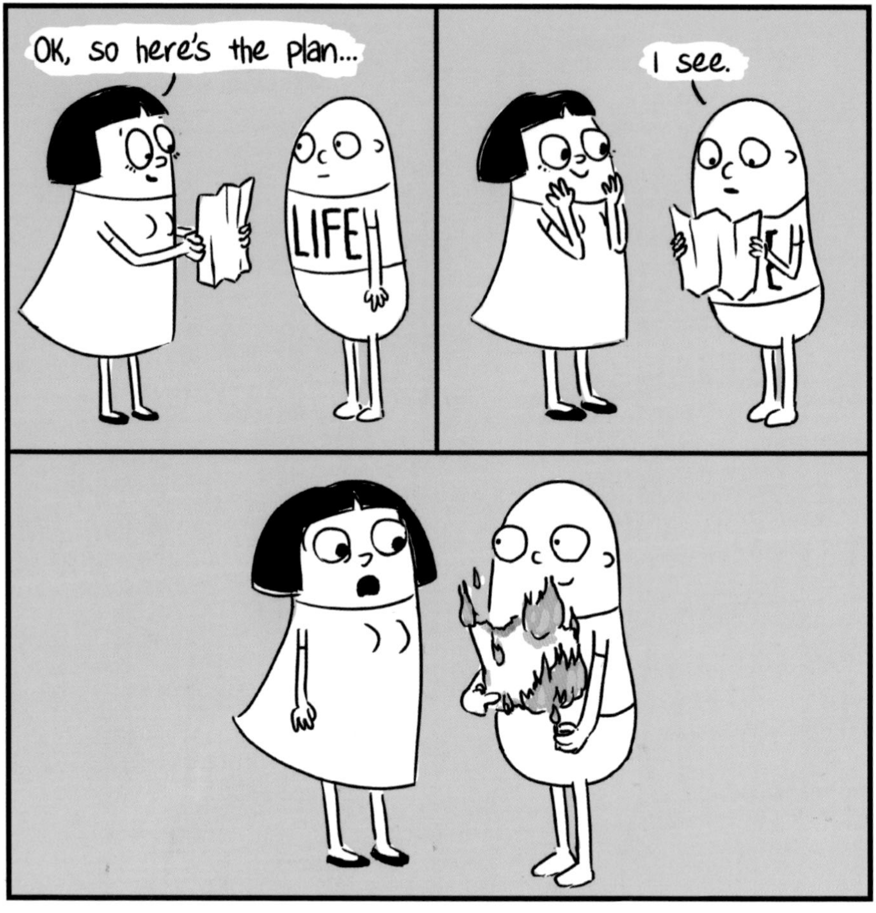
OK, so here's the plan...
LIFE
I see.

YOGA IS A GREAT WAY TO RELAX.

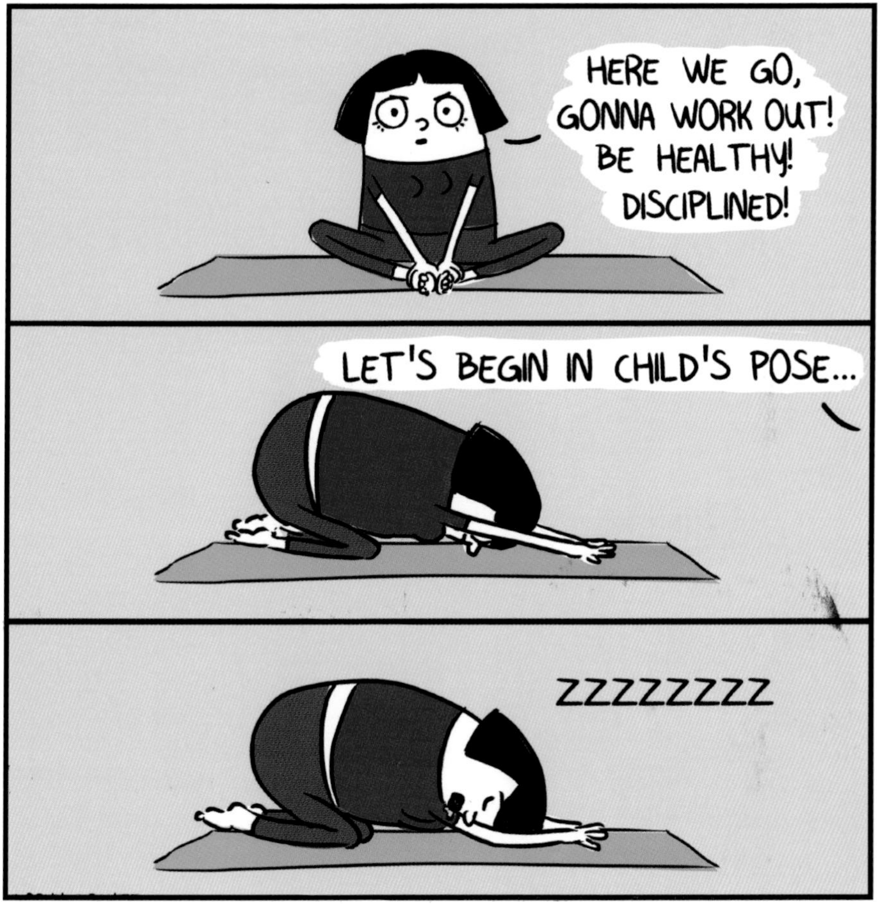
HERE WE GO, GONNA WORK OUT! BE HEALTHY! DISCIPLINED!
LET'S BEGIN IN CHILD'S POSE...
ZZZZZZZZ

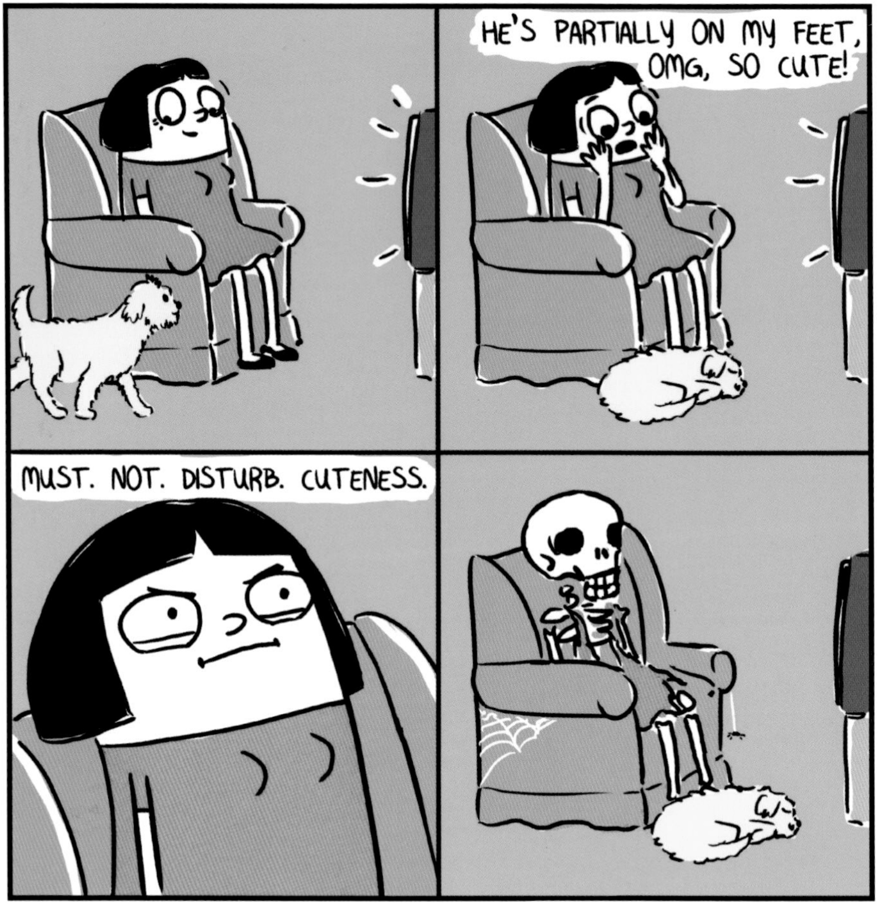
HE'S PARTIALLY ON MY FEET, OMG, SO CUTE!
MUST. NOT. DISTURB. CUTENESS.

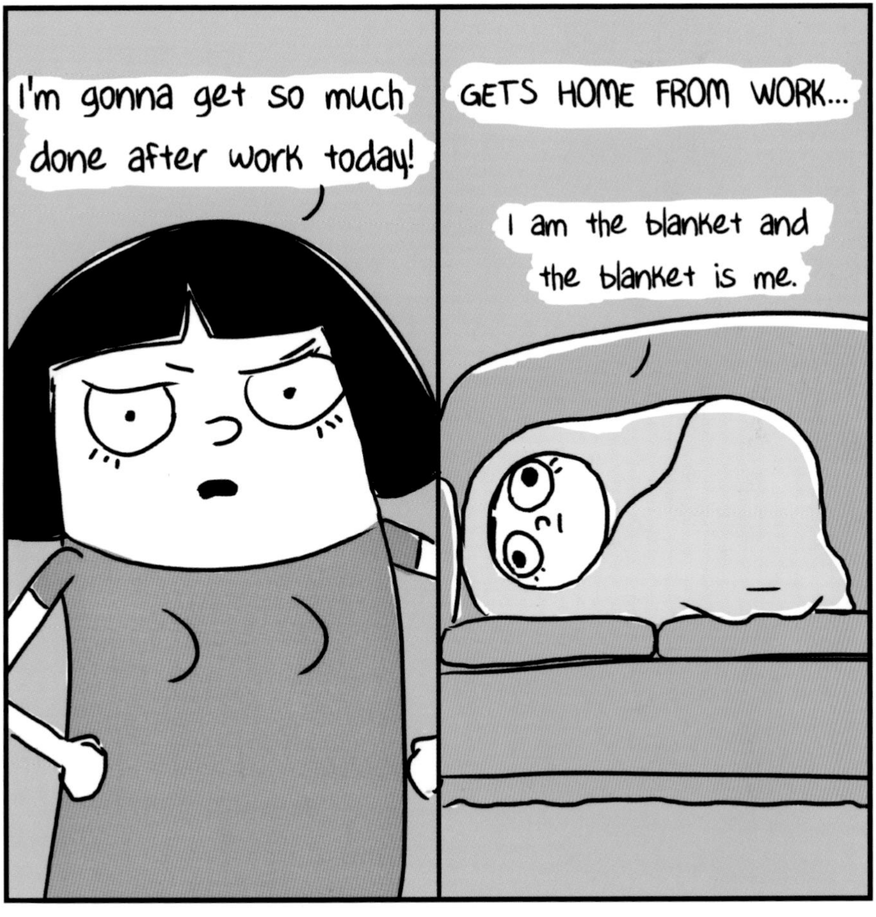
I'm gonna get so much done after work today!
GETS HOME FROM WORK...
I am the blanket and the blanket is me.

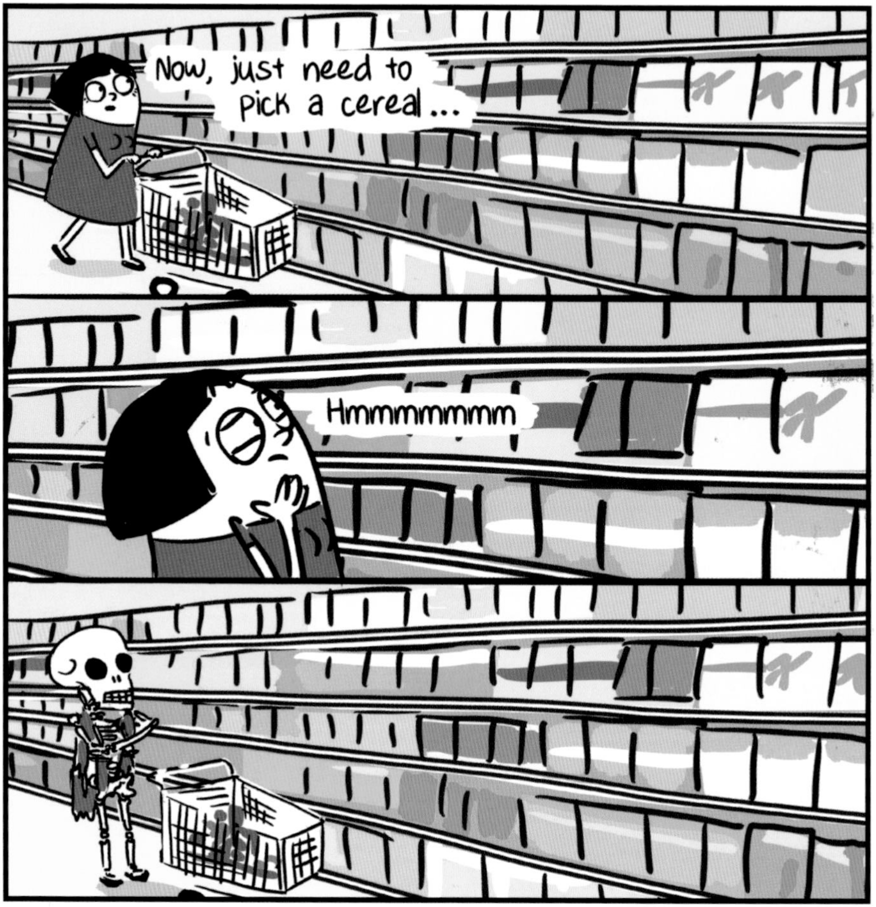
Now, just need to pick a cereal...
Hmmmmmmm

SHOOT FOR THE STARS.

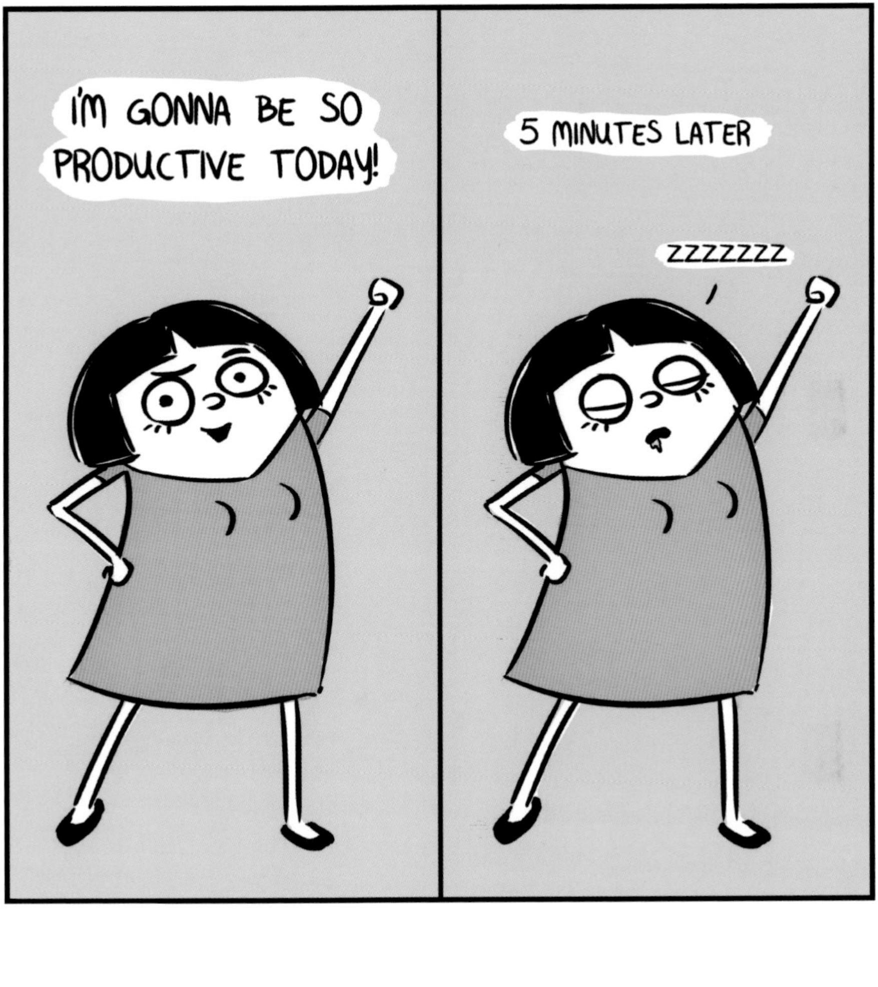
I'M GONNA BE SO PRODUCTIVE TODAY!
5 MINUTES LATER
ZZZZZZZ

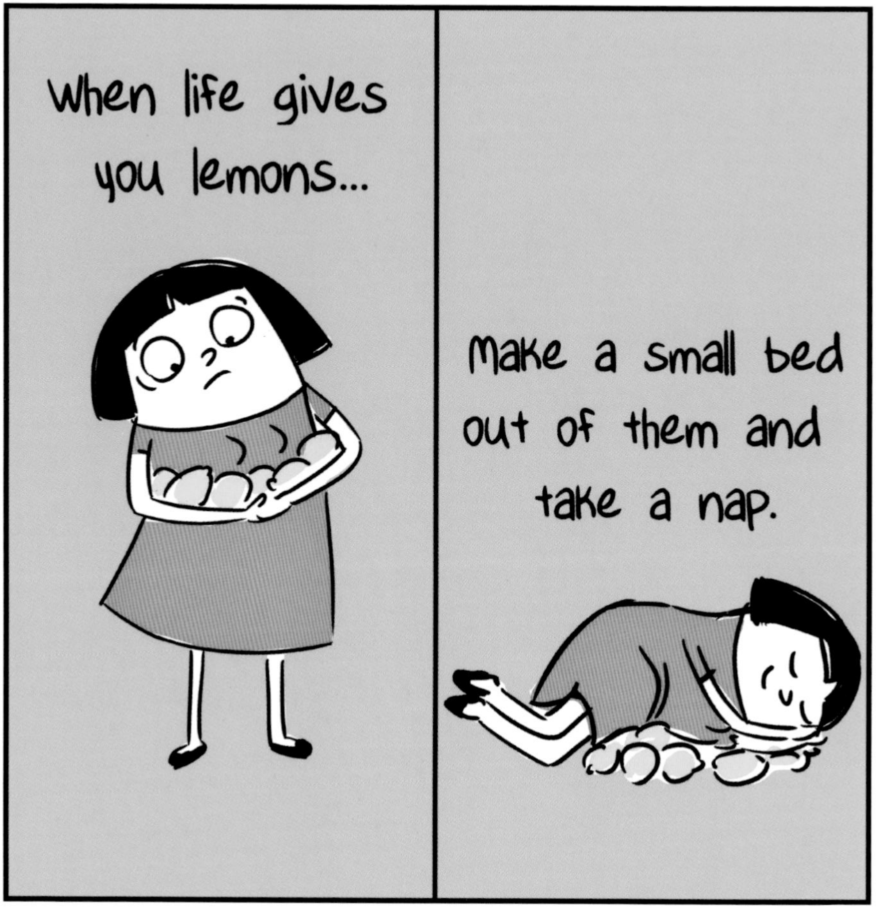
When life gives you lemons...
Make a small bed out of them and take a nap.

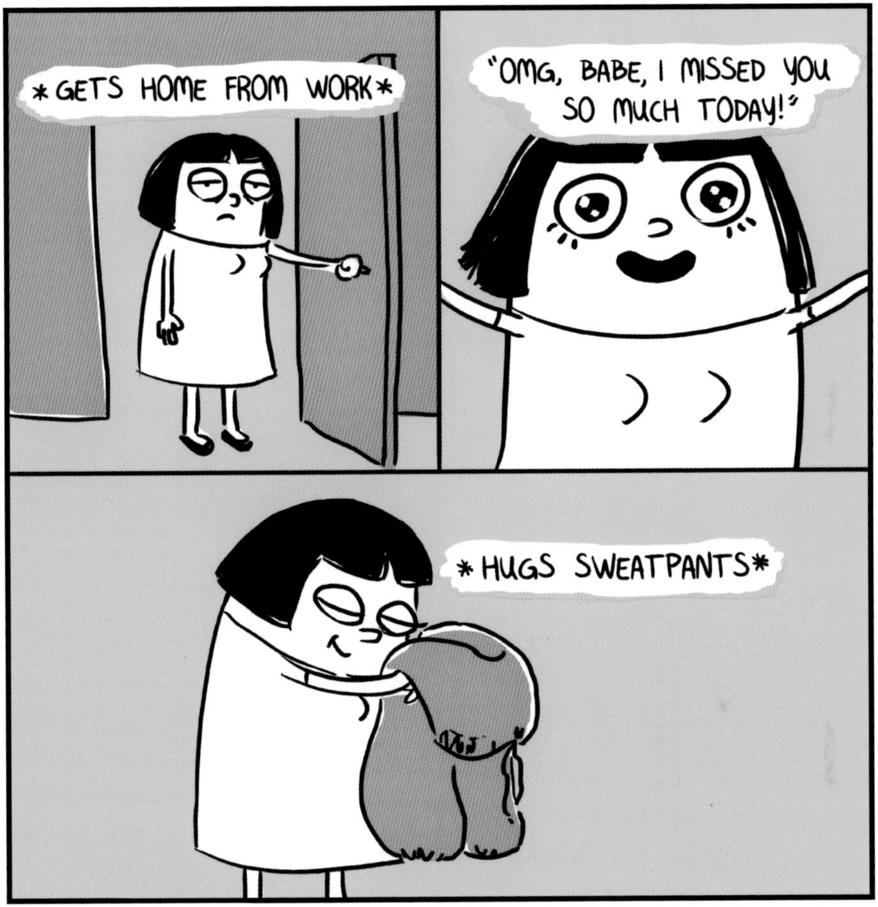
GETS HOME FROM WORK
"OMG, BABE, I MISSED YOU SO MUCH TODAY!"
HUGS SWEATPANTS

YOUR DREAMS ARE WITHIN REACH.

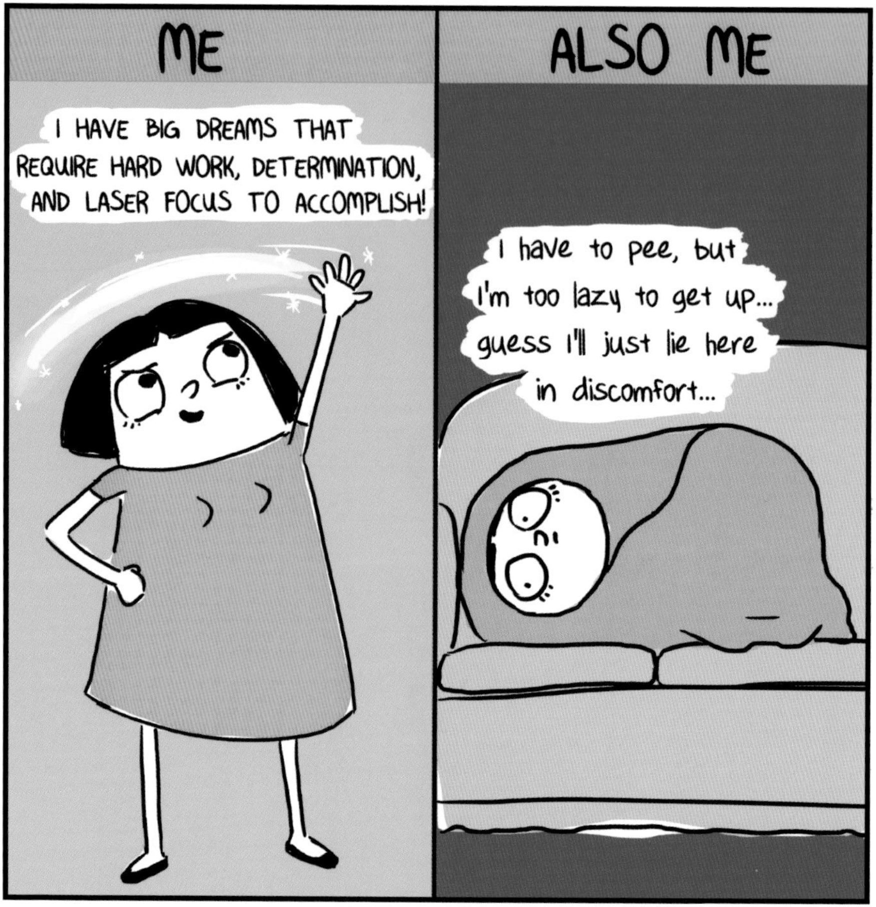
ME
I HAVE BIG DREAMS THAT REQUIRE HARD WORK, DETERMINATION, AND LASER FOCUS TO ACCOMPLISH!
ALSO ME
I have to pee, but I'm too lazy to get up... guess I'll just lie here in discomfort...

MATING HABITS

HOW TO DRIVE A MAN CRAZY
IN 10 SIMPLE STEPS

STEP 1:

Lightly scratch his scalp. The male's scalp is very sensitive.
This will send tingles down his spine.

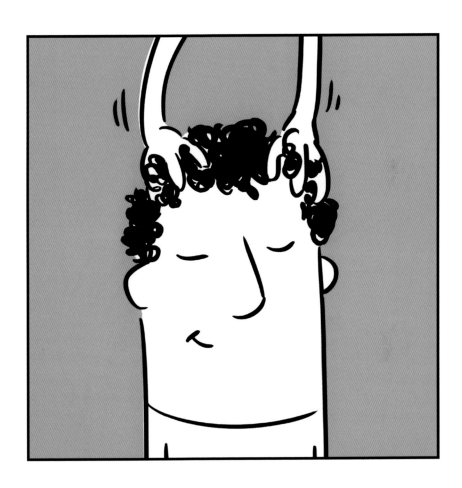

STEP 2:

Grab him and give him a gentle squeeze . . . GENTLE.
You have to be gentle because if you squeeze too hard,
he may find you threatening.

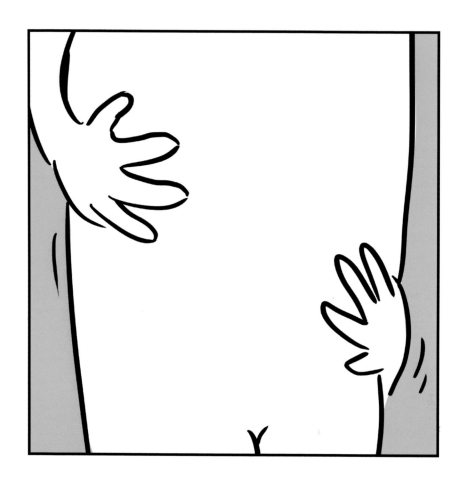

STEP 3:

Lightly spell out the word "GUAC" on his neck. Guac is widely considered the sexiest of all chip dips. Just spelling it with your fingers will send subliminal messages to his dick receptors.

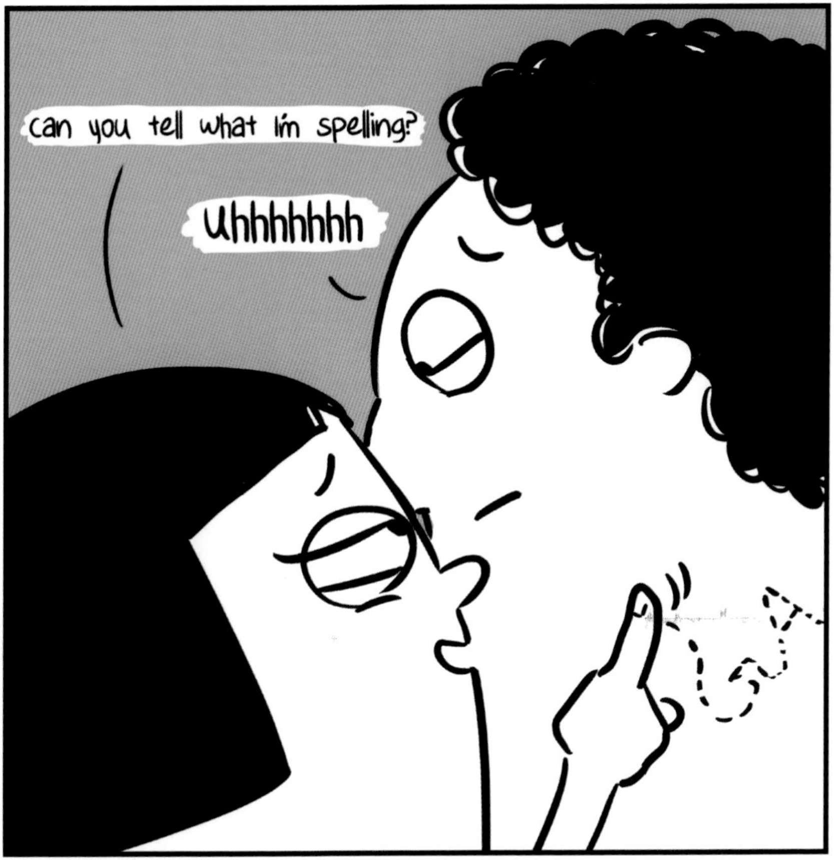

Can you tell what I'm spelling?
Uhhhhhhh

STEP 4:

Sexily rub guac between his toes. Men love to have smooshy stuff between their toes. It will remind him of standing on a giant jellyfish—doesn't get sexier than that.

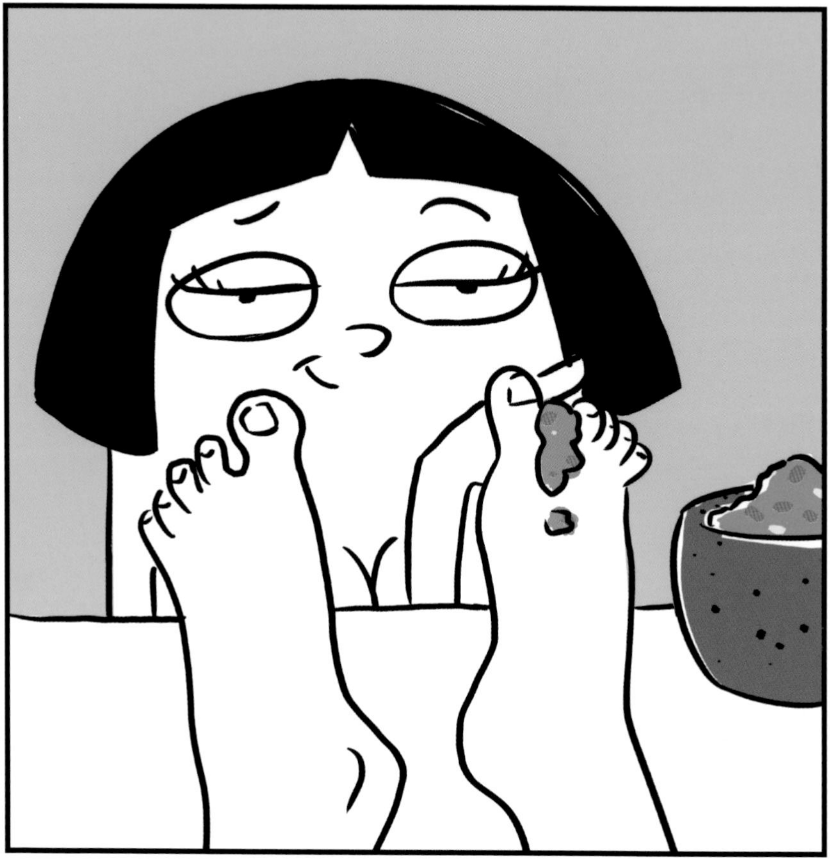

STEP 5:

very slowly dip a tortilla chip into the toe guac. Do this very slowly so you don't overwhelm him with too much sexiness at once.

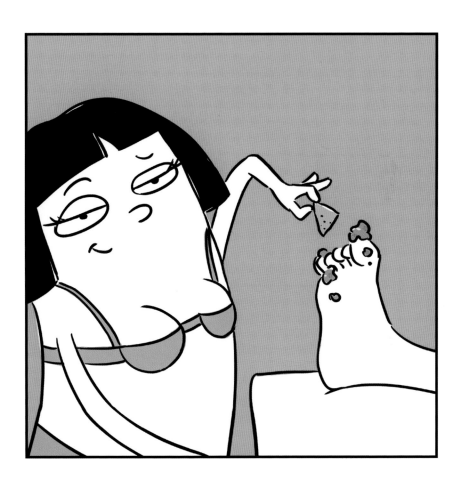

STEP 6:

While maintaining eye contact with him, seductively crawl over to him and offer the chip. The crawling will remind him of a female spider coming home to feed her young, and that will be a huge turn-on.

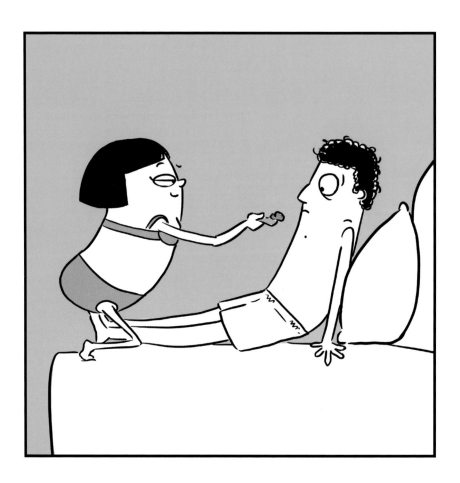

STEP 7:

While shushing him, gently press the chip onto his face, guac side down, of course. The guac will act as a sexy bonding agent to keep the chip adhered to his face.

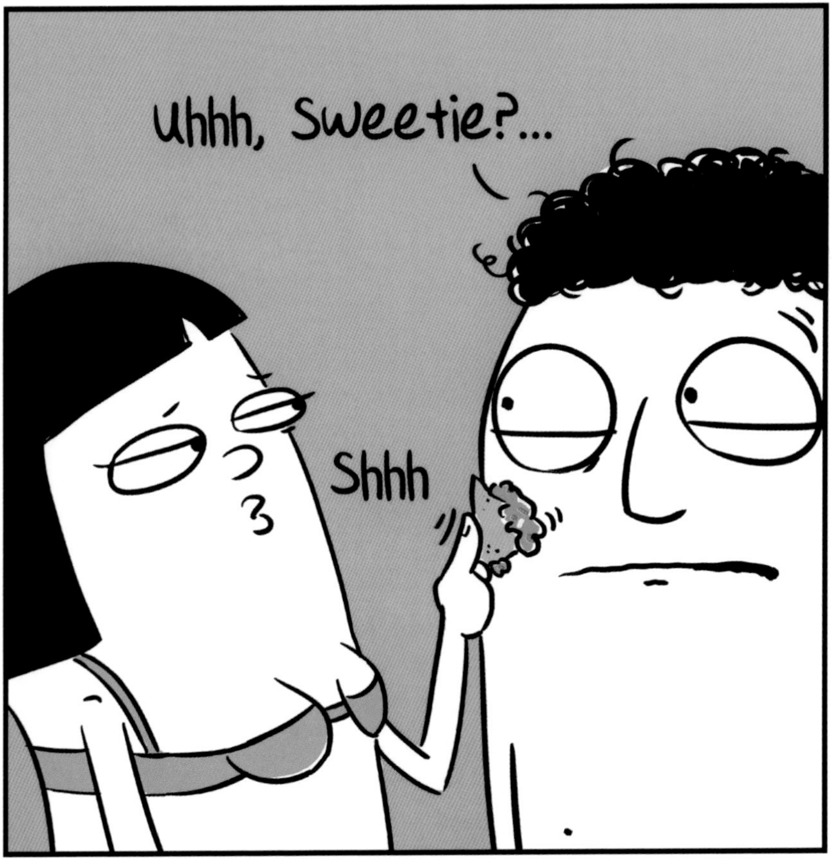
Uhhh, Sweetie?...
Shhh

STEP 8:

Give him a wink and reveal a single chunk of tomato from inside your bra. So mysterious, so sexy. "Where did this chunk come from?" and "How long has it been in her bra?" are some of the titillating questions he will be asking himself.

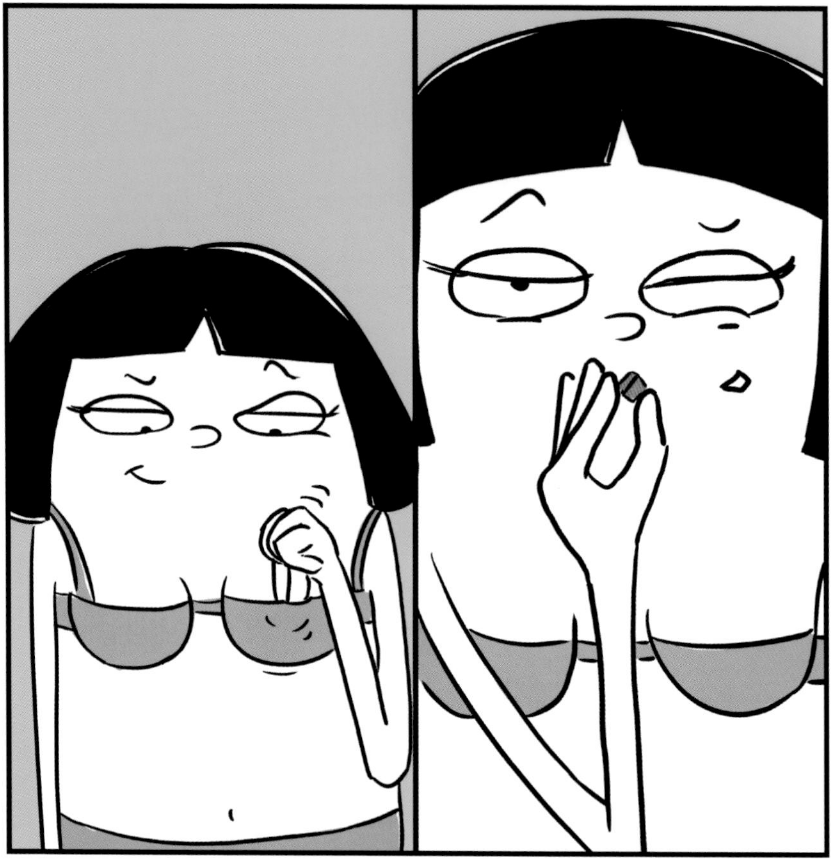

STEP 9:

Gingerly place the tomato chunk on the pillow next to his face.
GINGERLY!

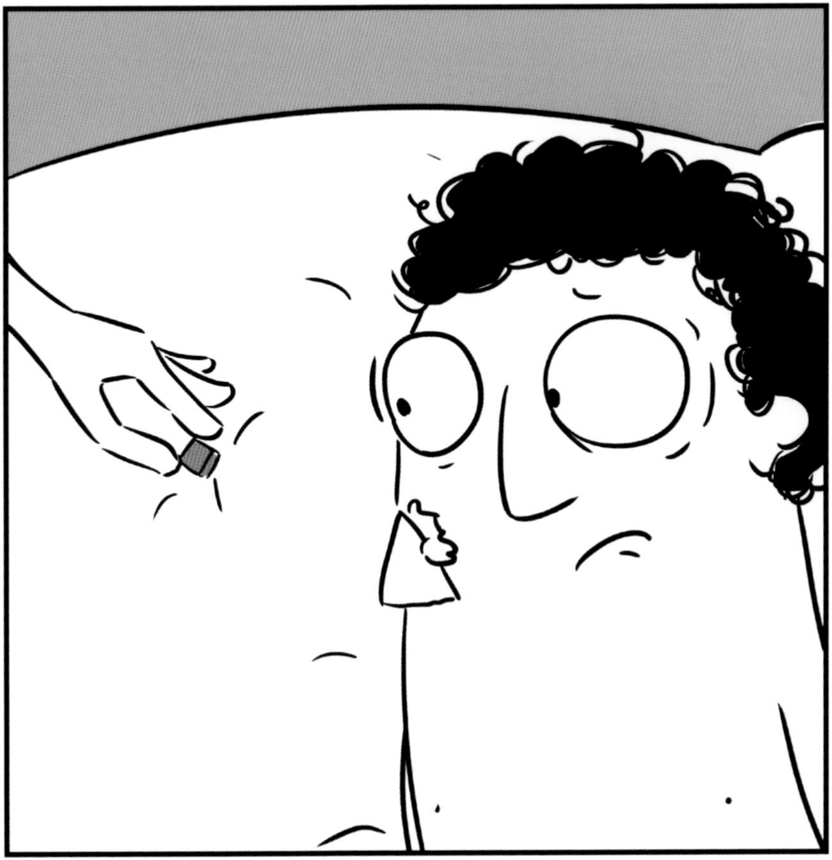

STEP 10:

Let the mysterious silence hang in the air as you slowly walk out the door. Right before you leave, pause and turn over your shoulder—quietly whisper "Guac . . . amole."

As you say "amole," he will orgasm instantaneously.

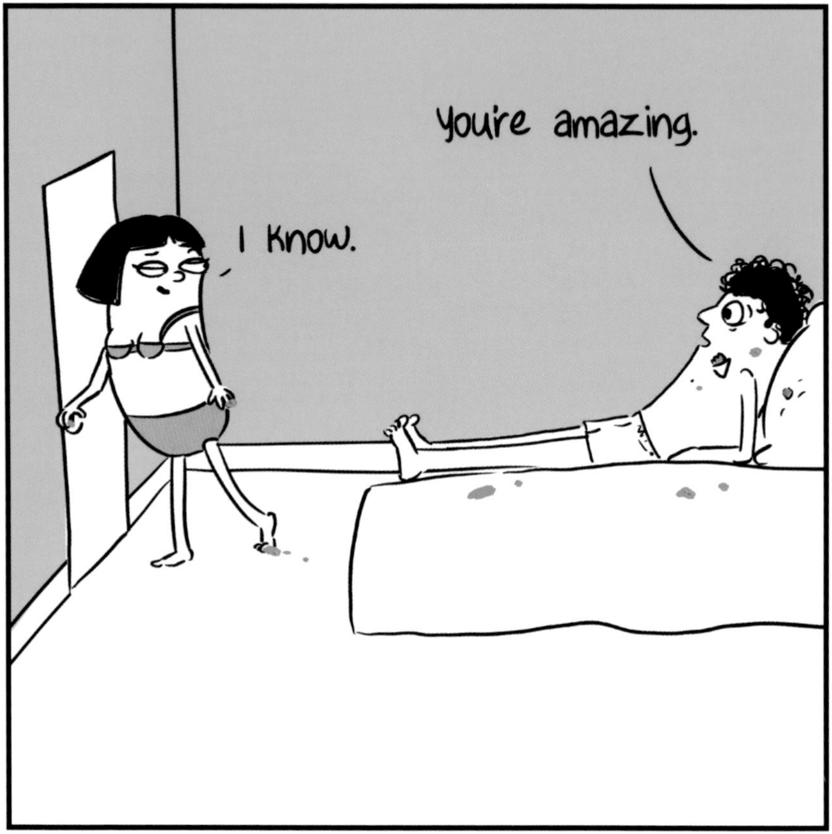
You're amazing.
I know.

THE END.

WHEN FLIRTING, ALWAYS BE YOURSELF.

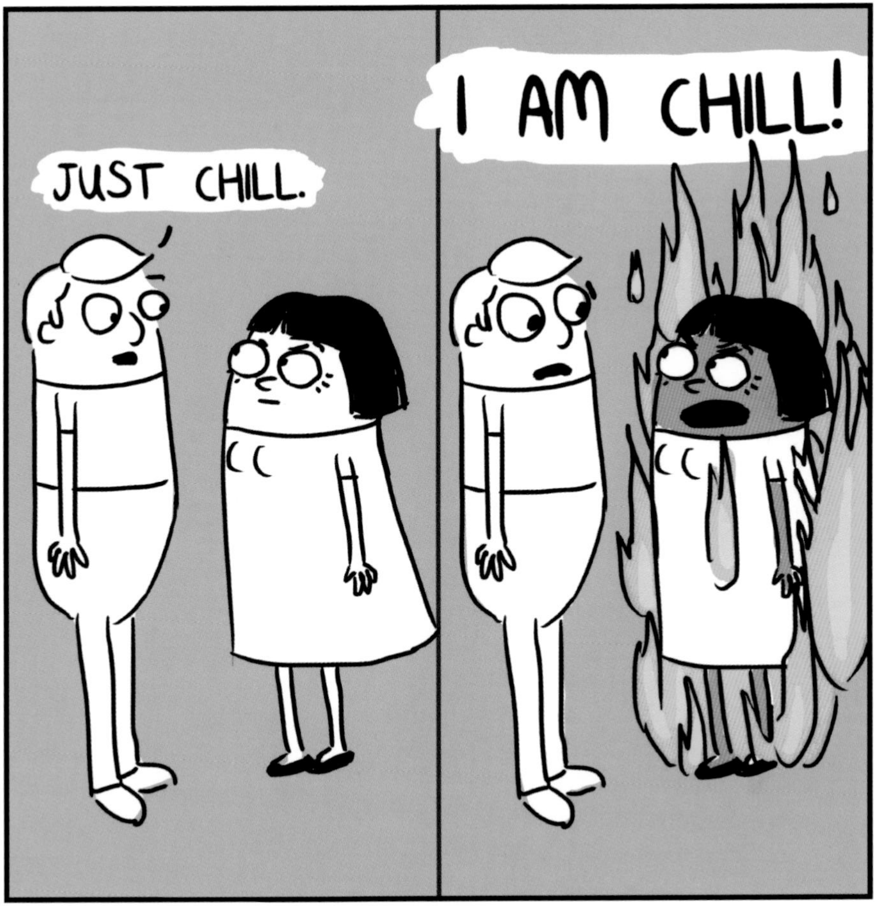
JUST CHILL.
I AM CHILL!

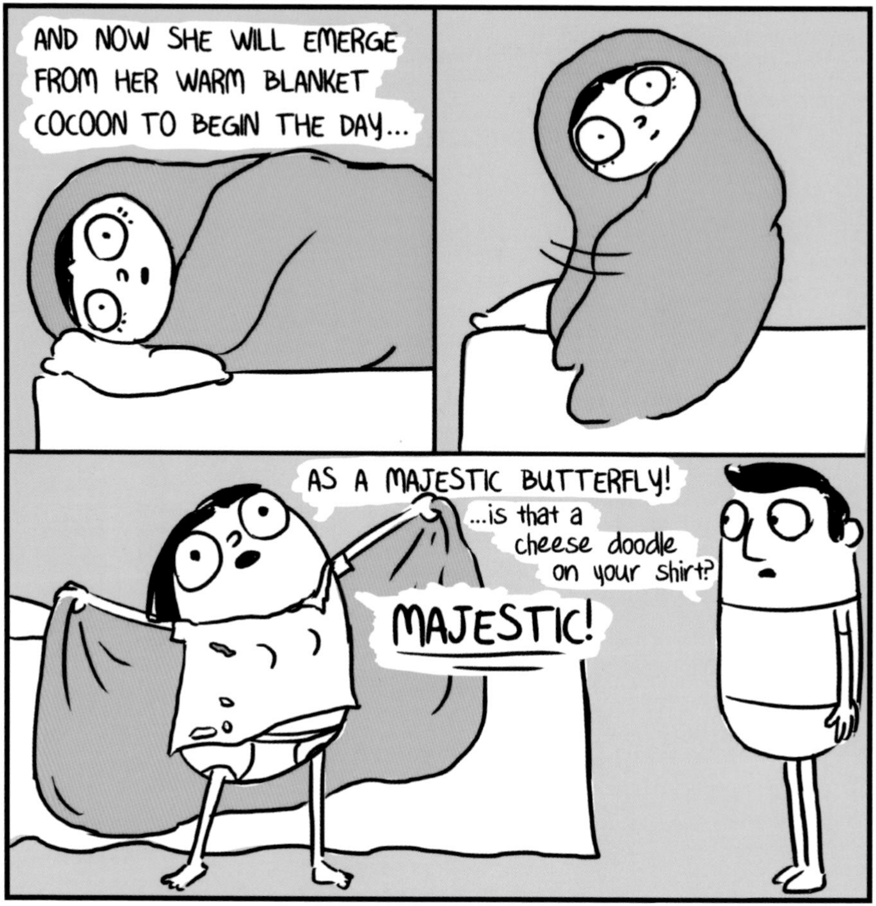
AND NOW SHE WILL EMERGE FROM HER WARM BLANKET COCOON TO BEGIN THE DAY...
AS A MAJESTIC BUTTERFLY!
...is that a cheese doodle on your shirt?
MAJESTIC!

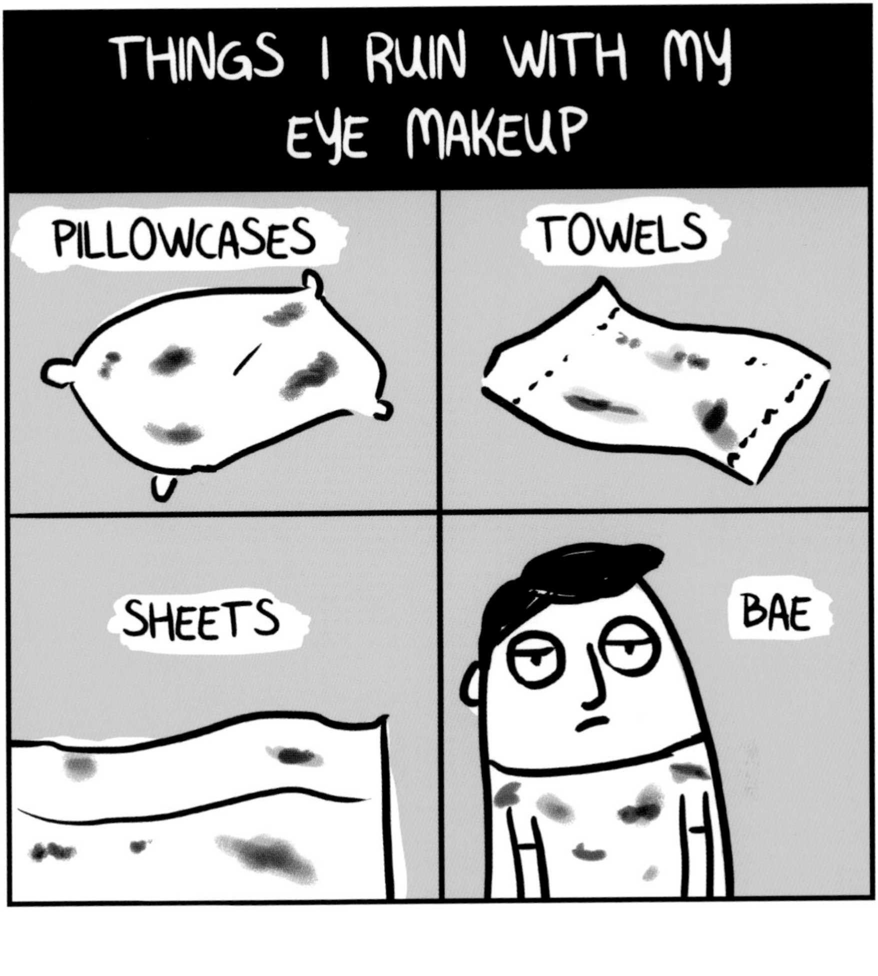
THINGS I RUIN WITH MY EYE MAKEUP
PILLOWCASES
TOWELS
SHEETS
BAE

THE BEDROOM CAN BE A BATTLEFIELD FOR SPACE.

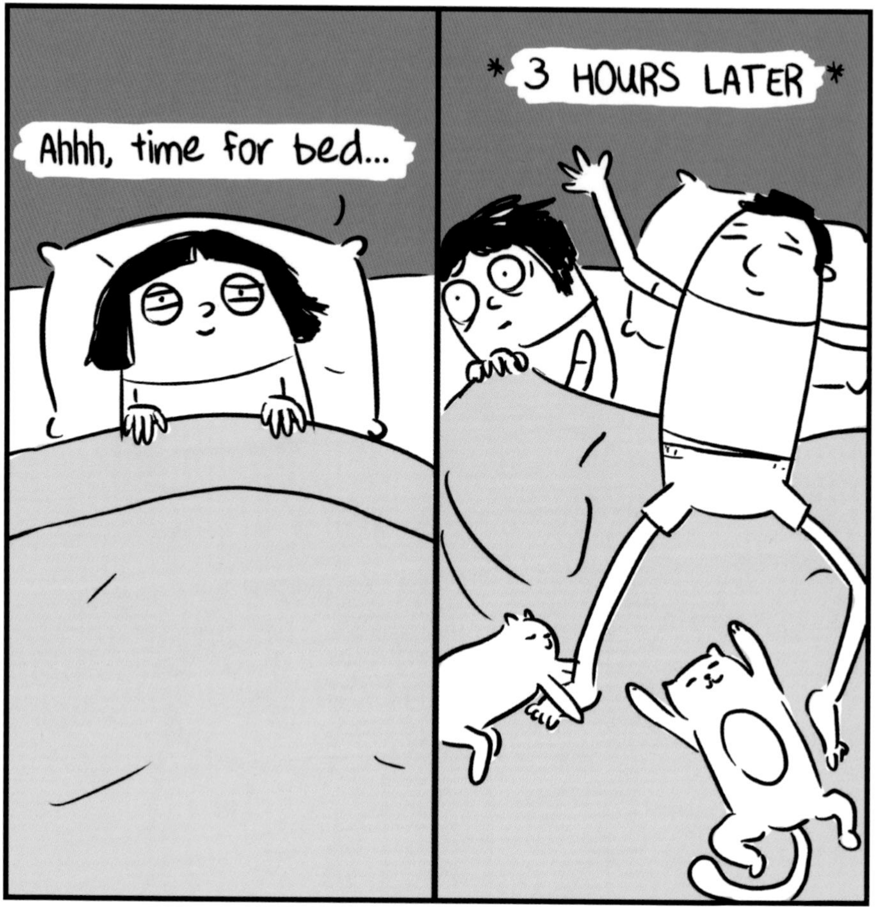
Ahhh, time for bed...
3 HOURS LATER

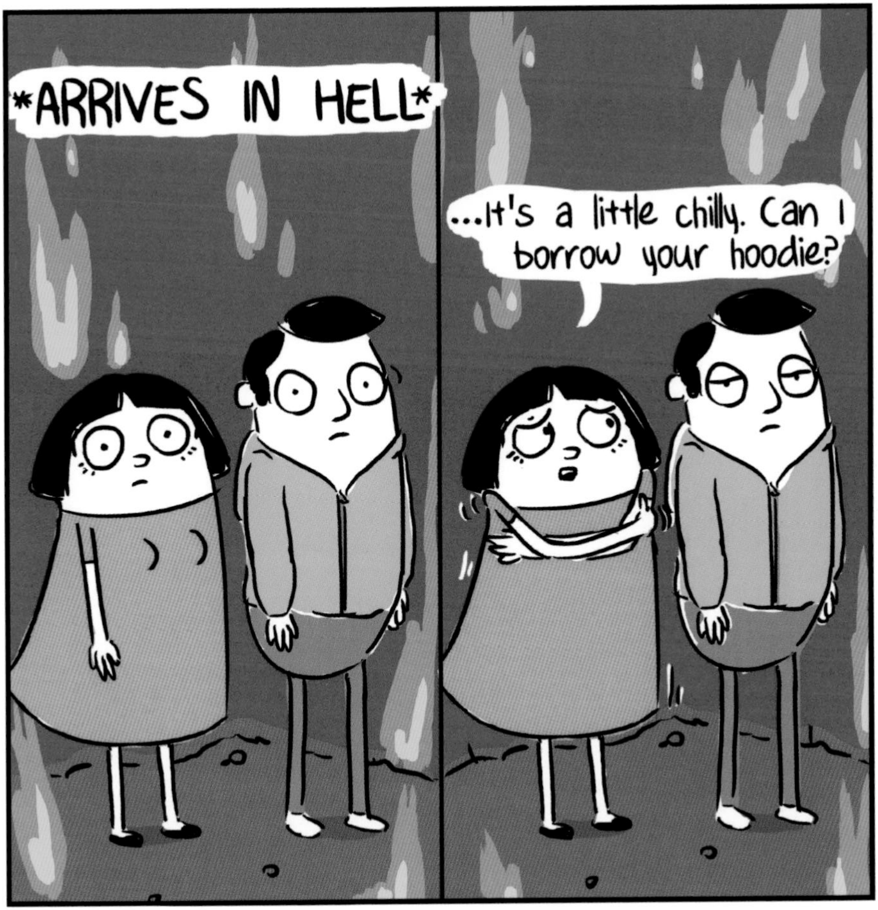
ARRIVES IN HELL
...It's a little chilly. Can I borrow your hoodie?

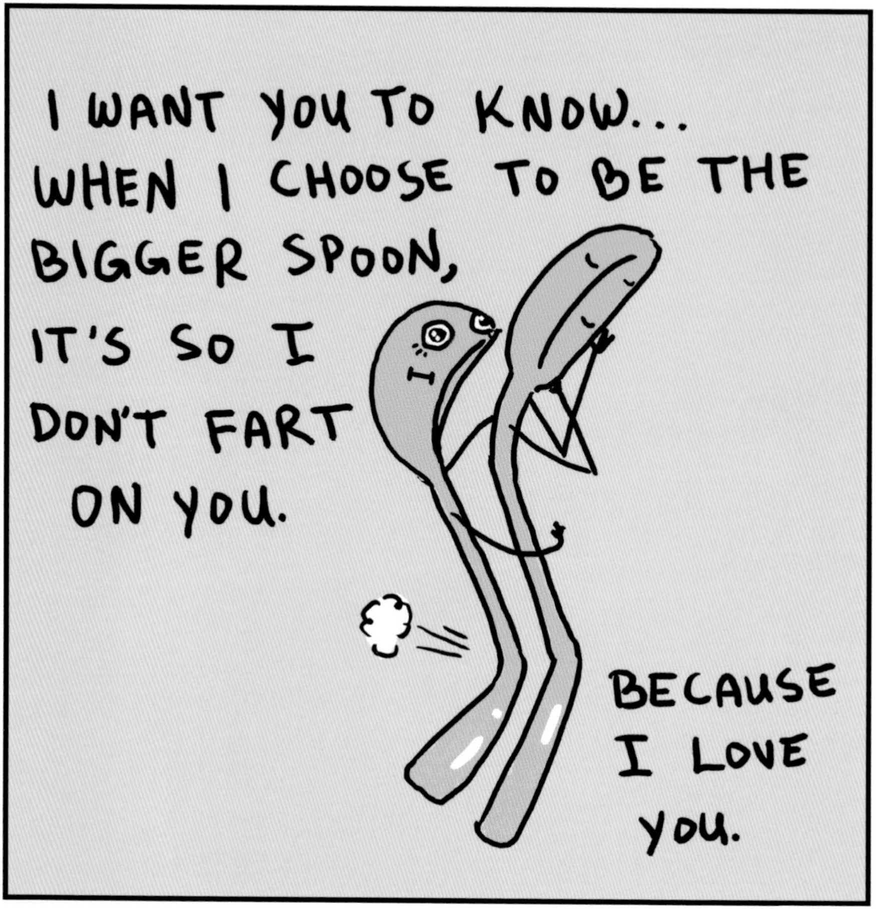
I WANT YOU TO KNOW...
WHEN I CHOOSE TO BE THE BIGGER SPOON,
IT'S SO I DON'T FART ON YOU.
BECAUSE I LOVE YOU.

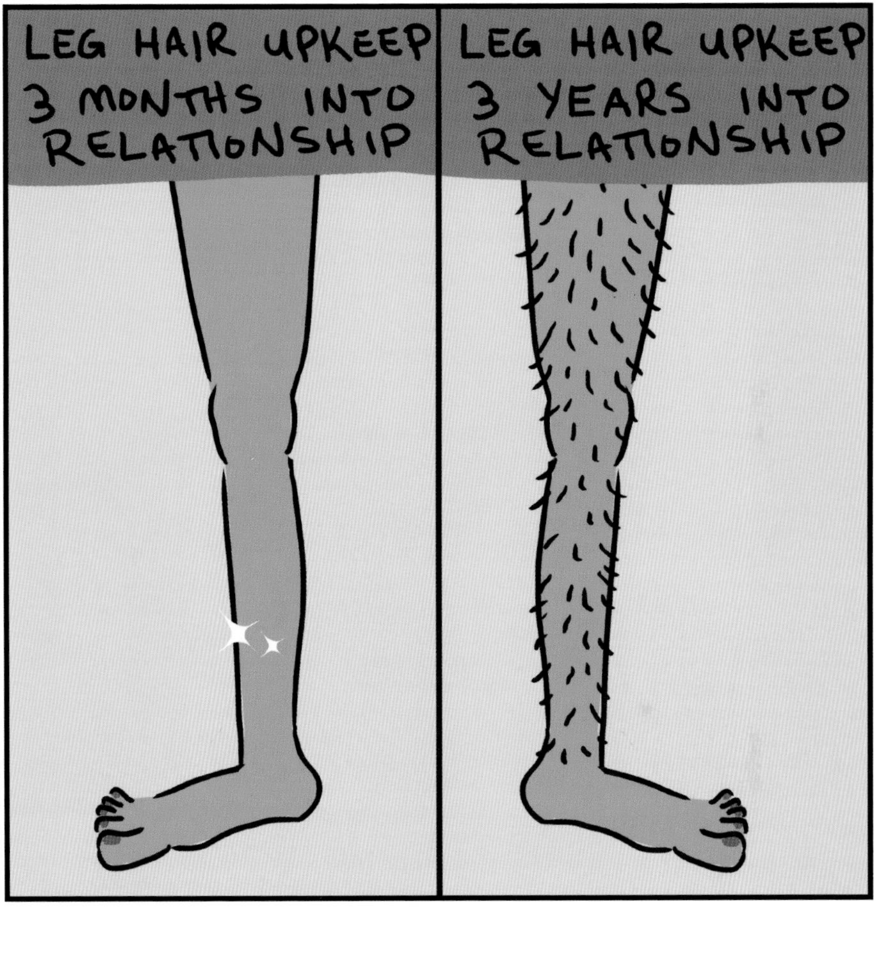
LEG HAIR UPKEEP 3 MONTHS INTO RELATIONSHIP
LEG HAIR UPKEEP 3 YEARS INTO RELATIONSHIP

FOR A HEALTHIER RELATIONSHIP, TAKE TURNS WITH CHORES.

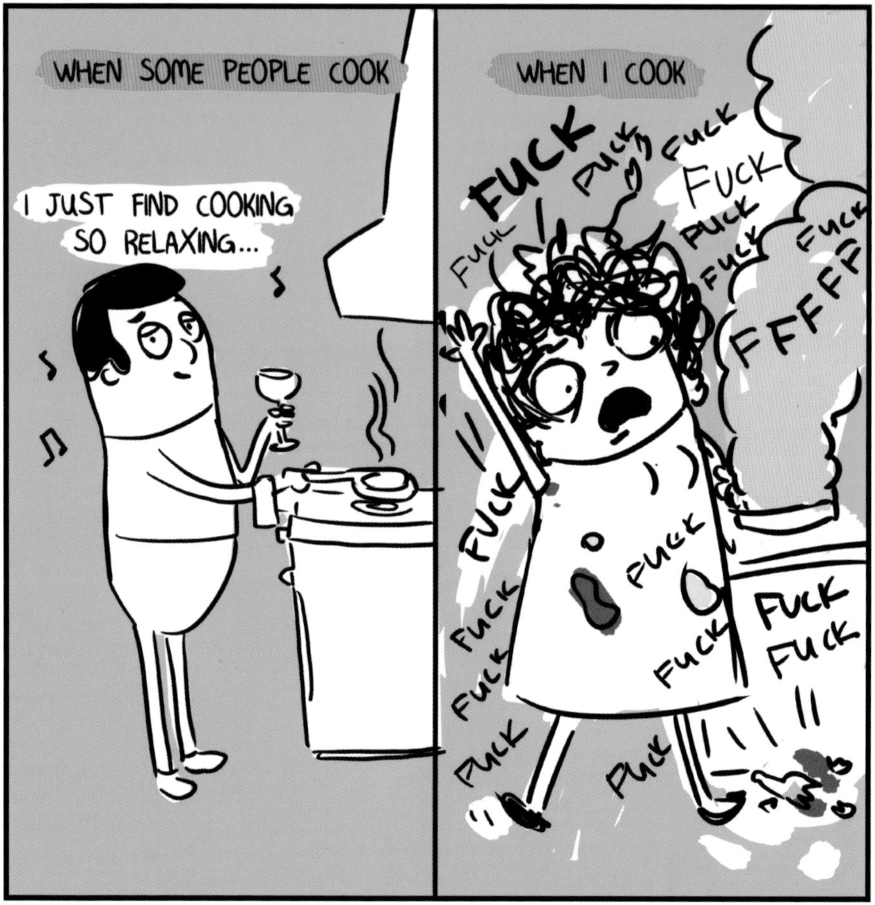
WHEN SOME PEOPLE COOK
I JUST FIND COOKING SO RELAXING...
WHEN I COOK
FUCK
FUCK
FUCK
FUCK
FUCK
FUCK
FUCK
FUCK
FFFFF
FUCK
FUCK
FUCK
FUCK
FUCK
FUCK
FUCK
FUCK
FUCK

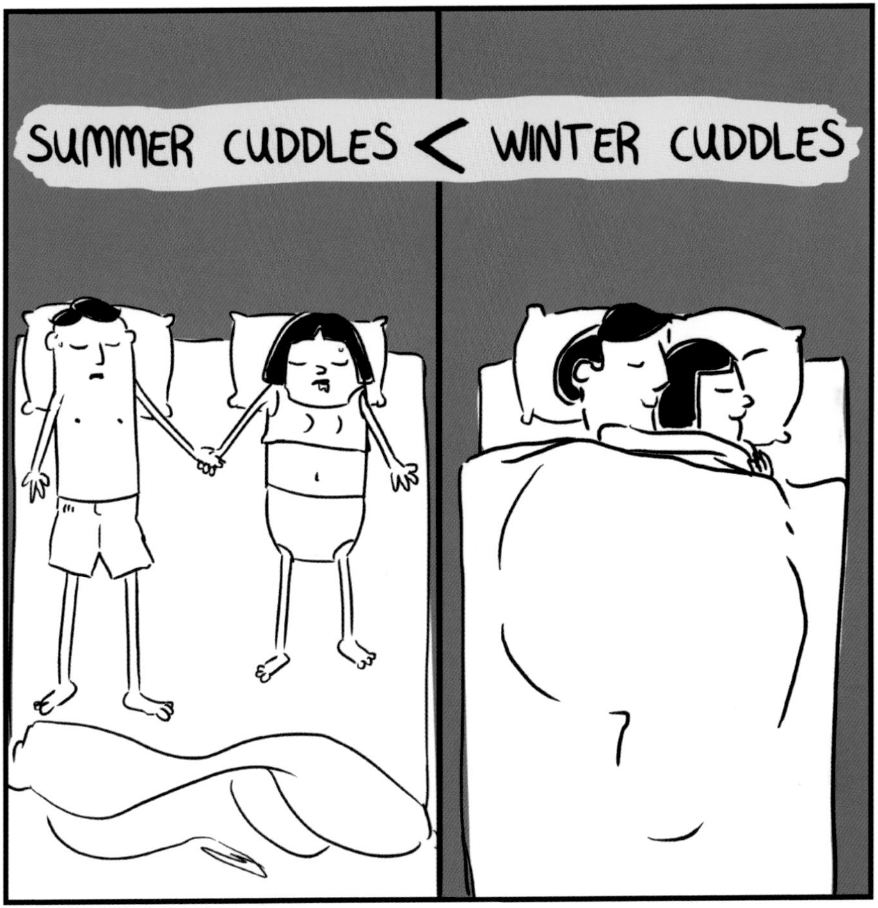
SUMMER CUDDLES < WINTER CUDDLES

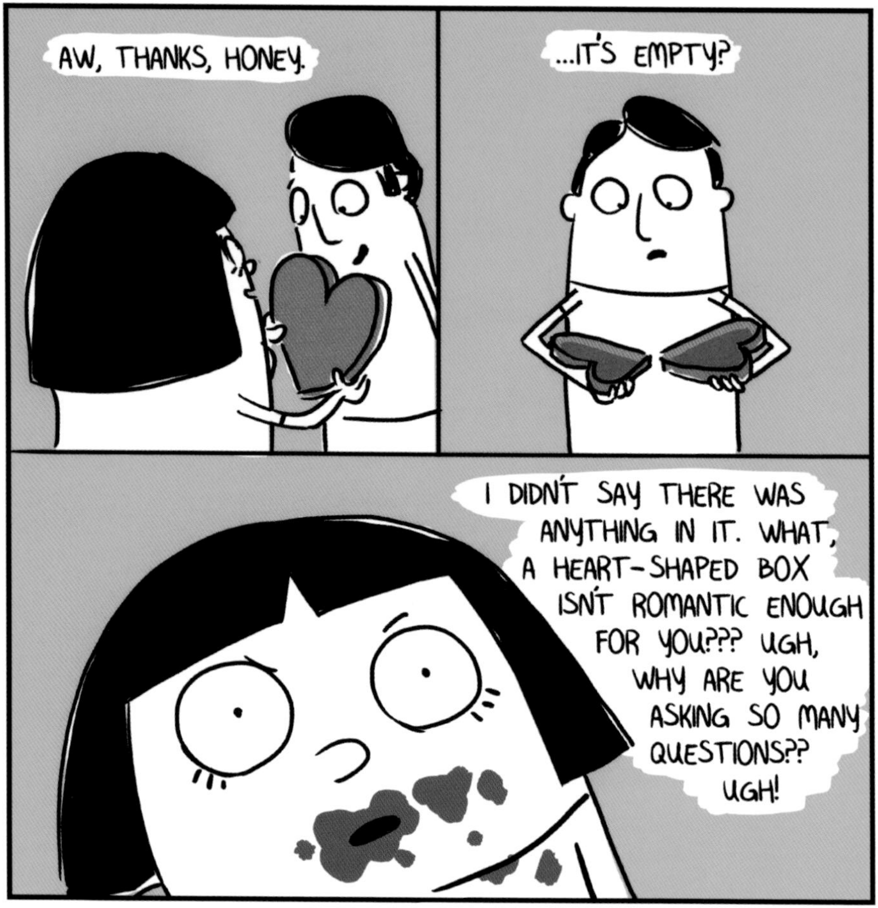
AW, THANKS, HONEY.
...IT'S EMPTY?
I DIDN'T SAY THERE WAS ANYTHING IN IT. WHAT, A HEART-SHAPED BOX ISN'T ROMANTIC ENOUGH FOR YOU??? UGH, WHY ARE YOU ASKING SO MANY QUESTIONS?? UGH!

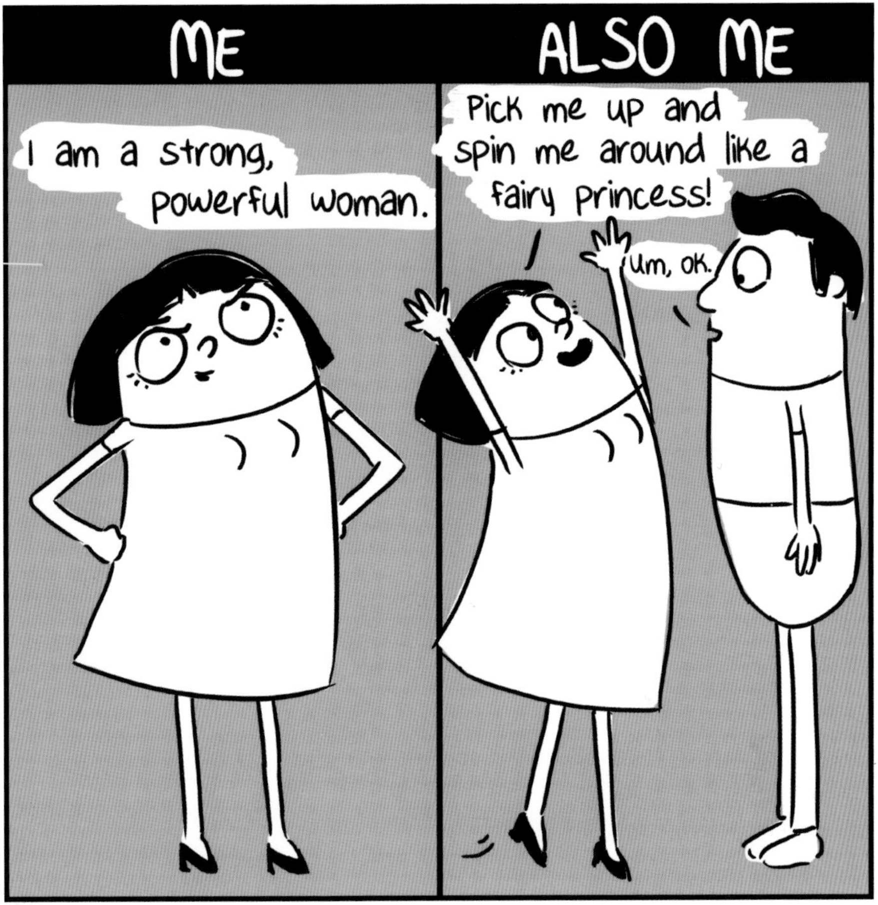
ME
ALSO ME
I am a strong, powerful woman.
Pick me up and spin me around like a fairy princess!
Um, OK.

LOVE CAN MAKE YOU FEEL LIKE YOU'RE FLOATING ON AIR.

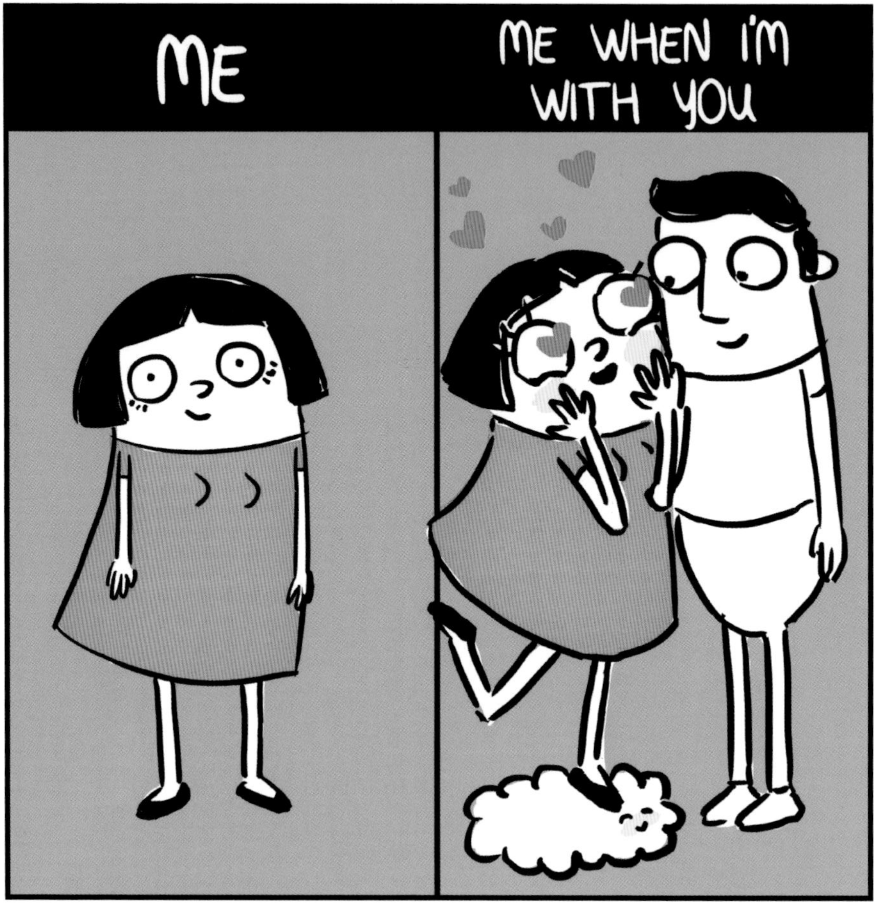
ME
ME WHEN I'M WITH YOU

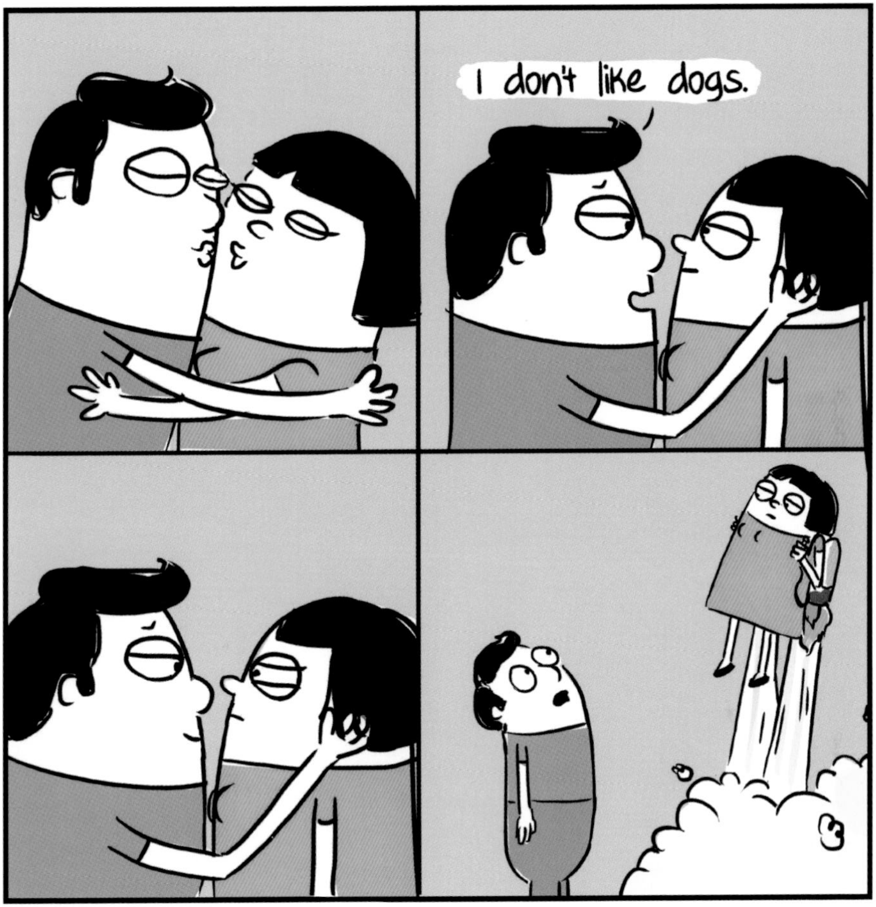
I don't like dogs.

OVER TIME YOUR RELATIONSHIP WILL GO TO NEW AND EXCITING PLACES.

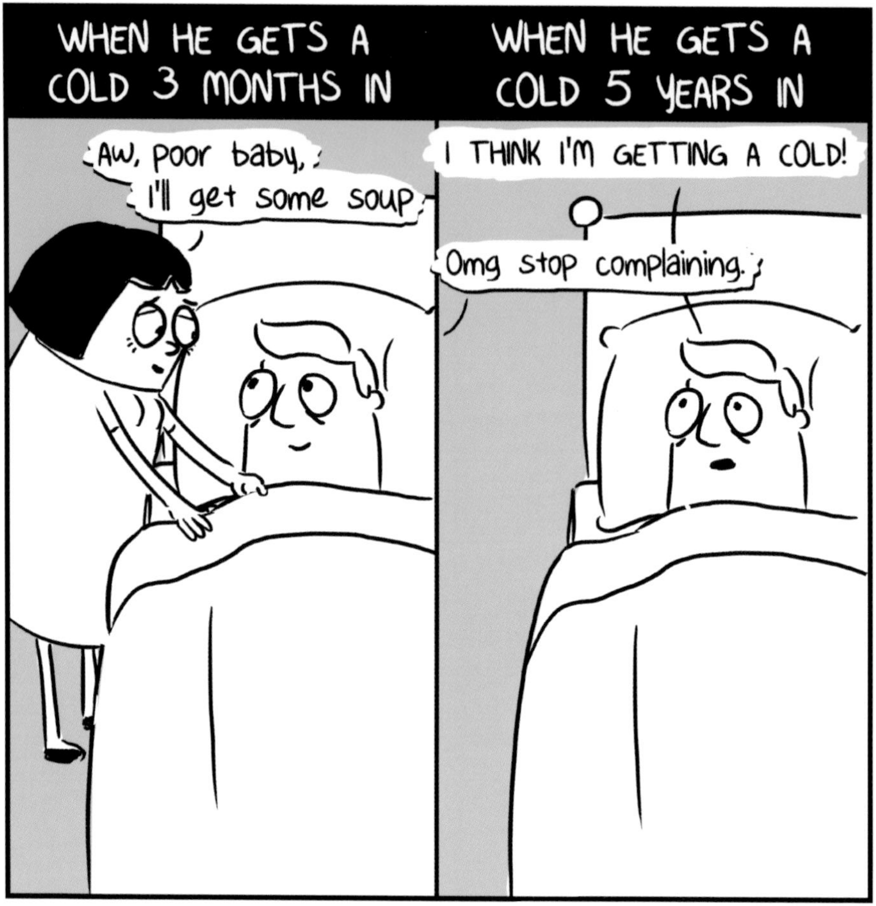
WHEN HE GETS A COLD 3 MONTHS IN
Aw, poor baby,
I'll get some soup
WHEN HE GETS A COLD 5 YEARS IN
I THINK I'M GETTING A COLD!
Omg stop complaining.

SELF-CARE

ALWAYS GET A GOOD NIGHT'S SLEEP.

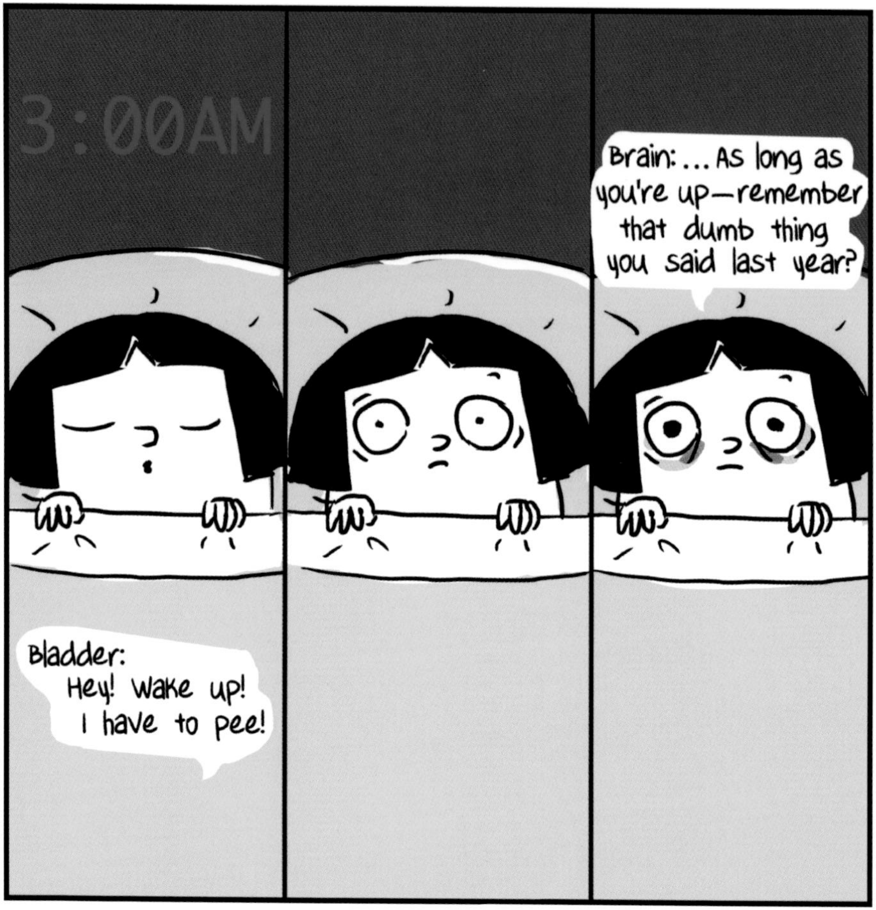
3:00AM
Bladder: Hey! Wake up! I have to pee!
Brain: ... As long as you're up—remember that dumb thing you said last year?

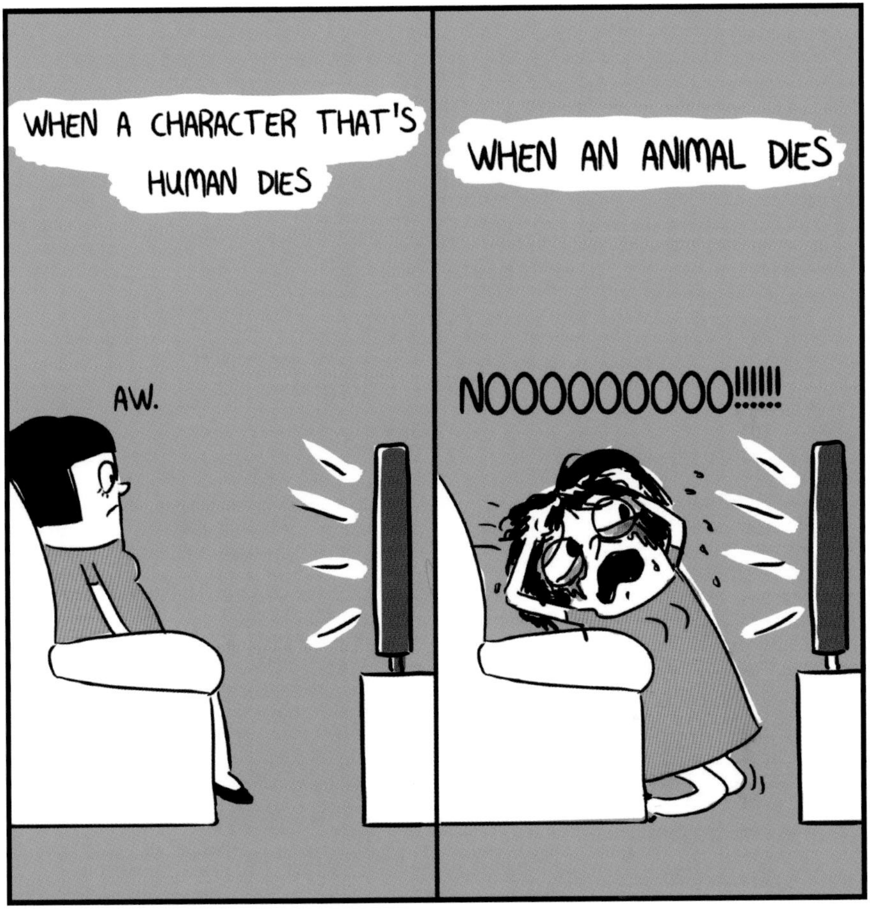
WHEN A CHARACTER THAT'S HUMAN DIES
AW.
WHEN AN ANIMAL DIES
NOOOOOOOOOO!!!!!!

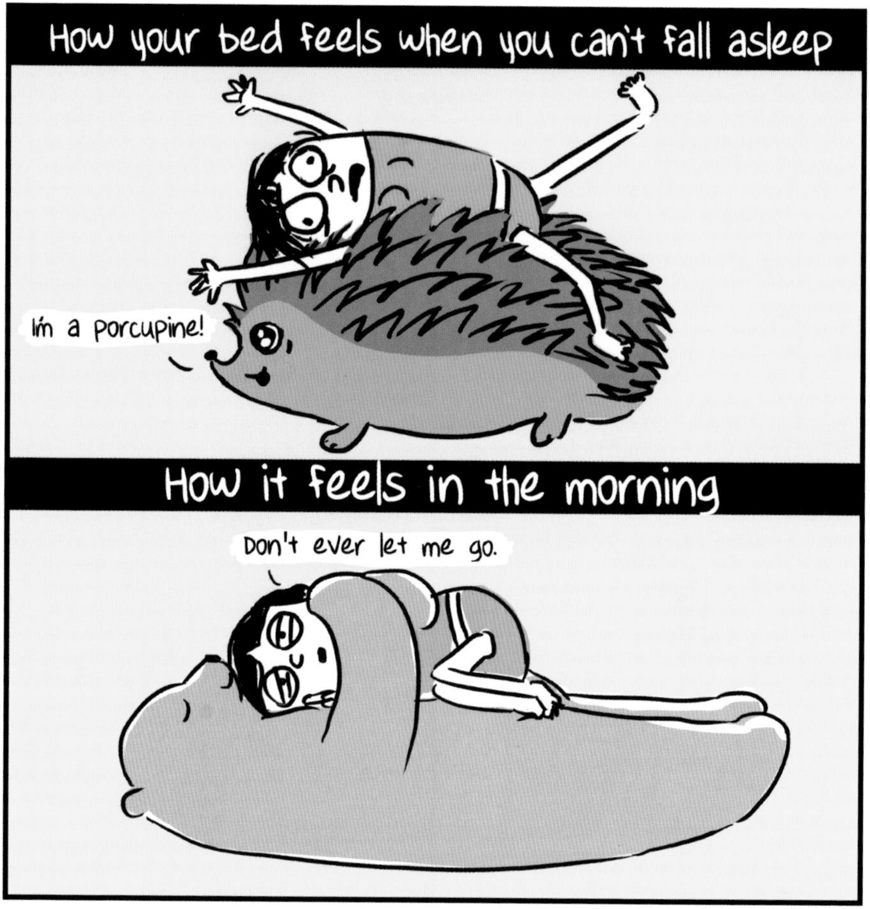
How your bed feels when you can't fall asleep
I'm a porcupine!
How it feels in the morning
Don't ever let me go.

WHEN IN DOUBT, HUG A FUZZY FRIEND.

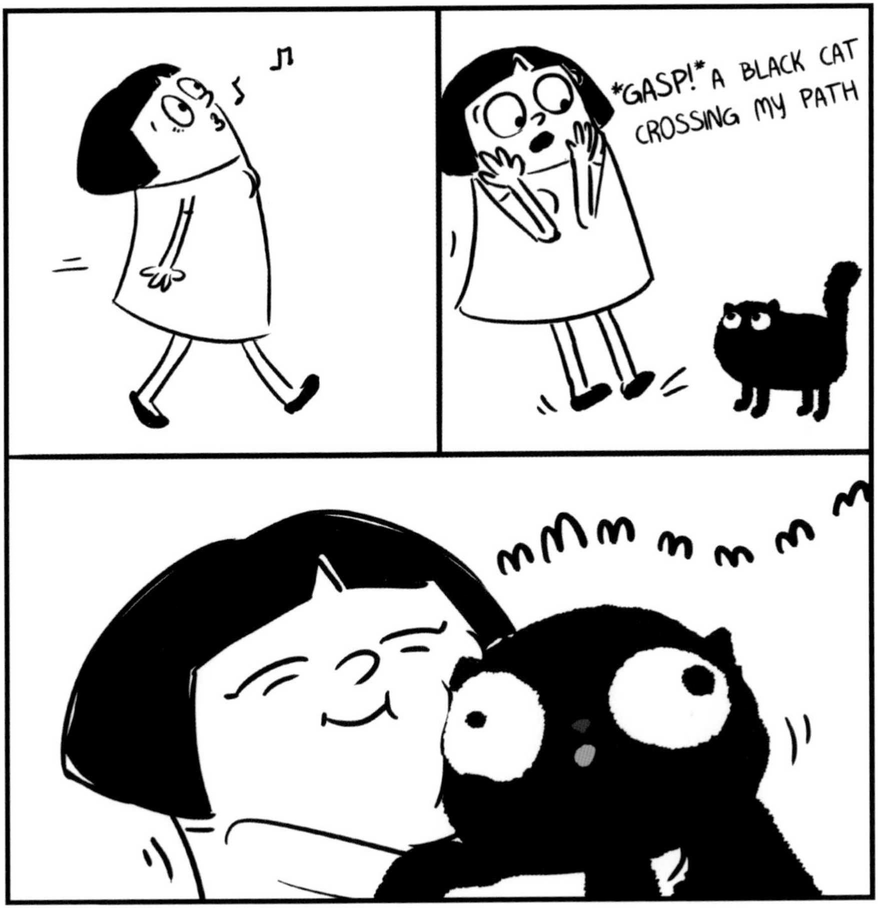
GASP! A BLACK CAT CROSSING MY PATH
mMmm m m m m

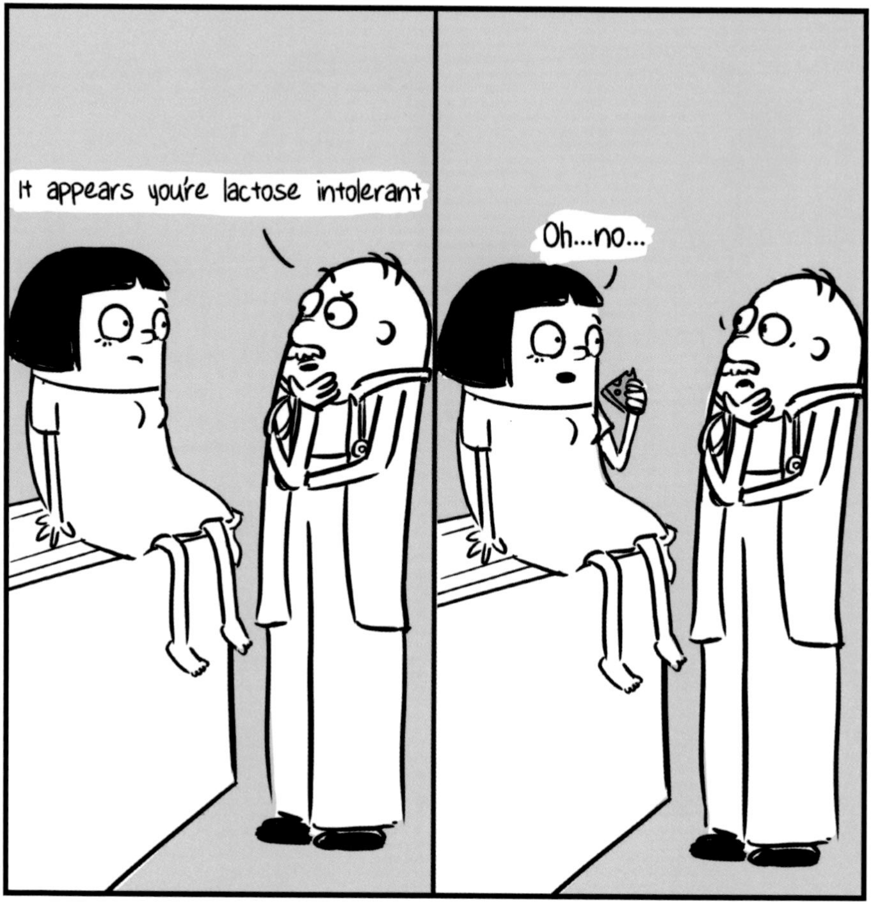
It appears you're lactose intolerant
Oh...no...

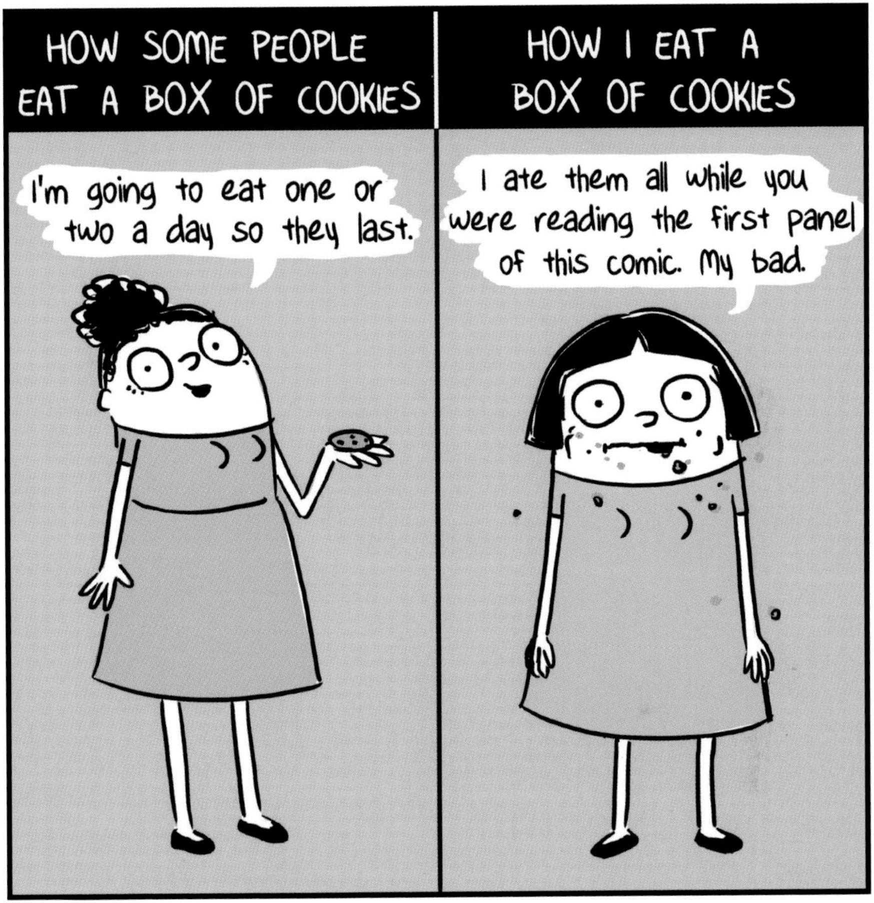
HOW SOME PEOPLE EAT A BOX OF COOKIES
I'm going to eat one or two a day so they last.
HOW I EAT A BOX OF COOKIES
I ate them all while you were reading the first panel of this comic. My bad.

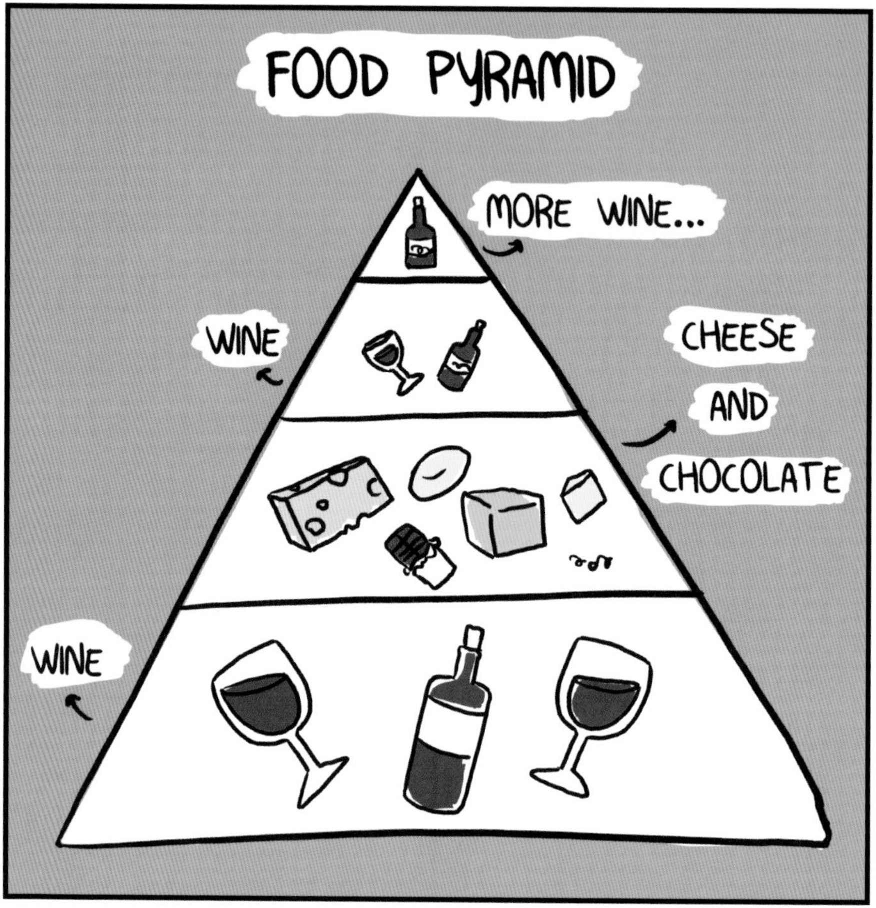
FOOD PYRAMID
MORE WINE...
WINE
CHEESE
AND
CHOCOLATE
WINE

NOT ALL LADIES GET PERIODS, BUT IF YOU DO, BEWARE OF CUTE CLOUDS.

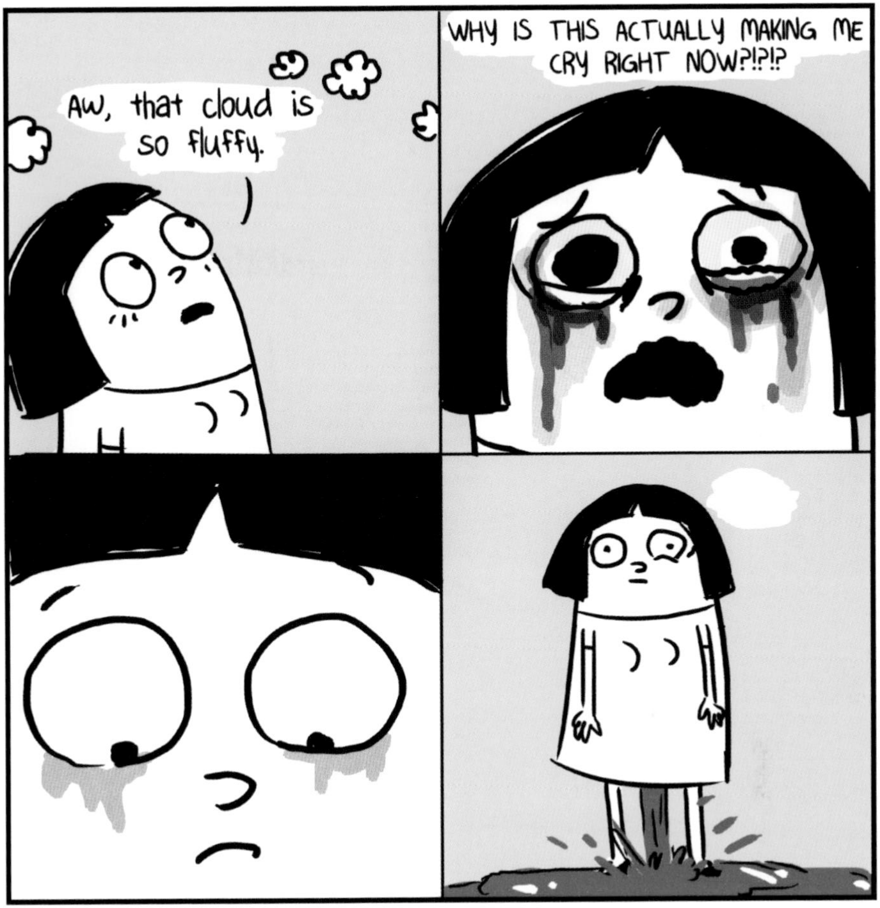
Aw, that cloud is so fluffy.
WHY IS THIS ACTUALLY MAKING ME CRY RIGHT NOW?!?!?

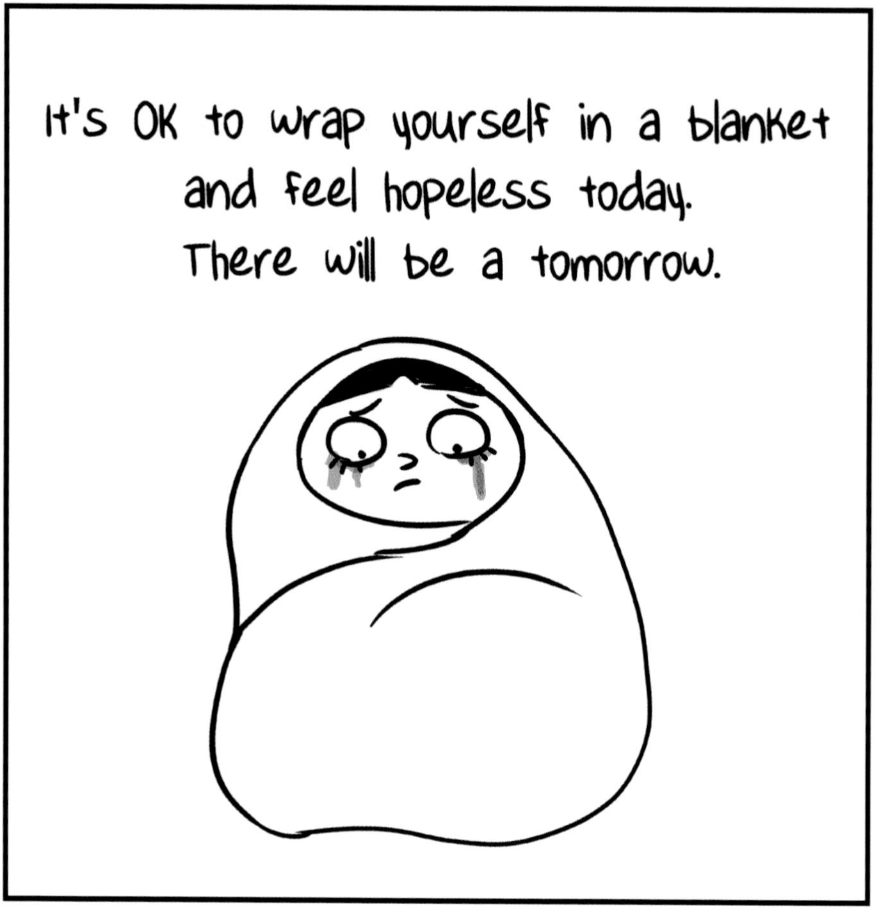
It's OK to wrap yourself in a blanket and feel hopeless today.
There will be a tomorrow.

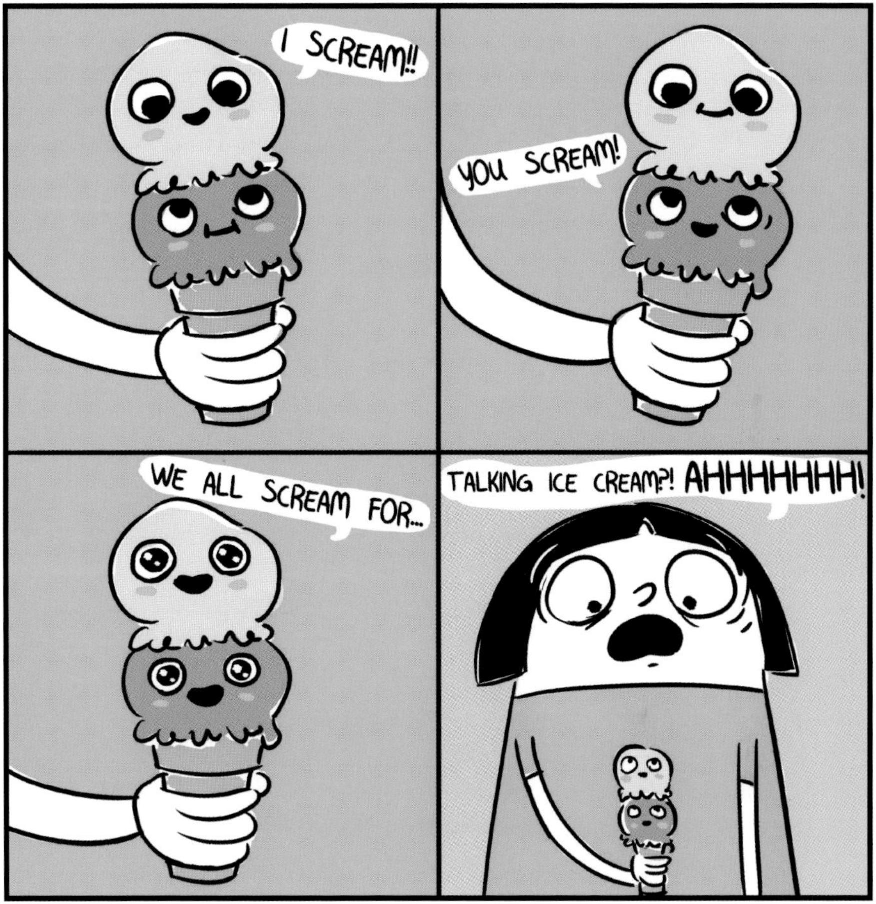
I SCREAM!!
YOU SCREAM!
WE ALL SCREAM FOR...
TALKING ICE CREAM?! AHHHHHHH!

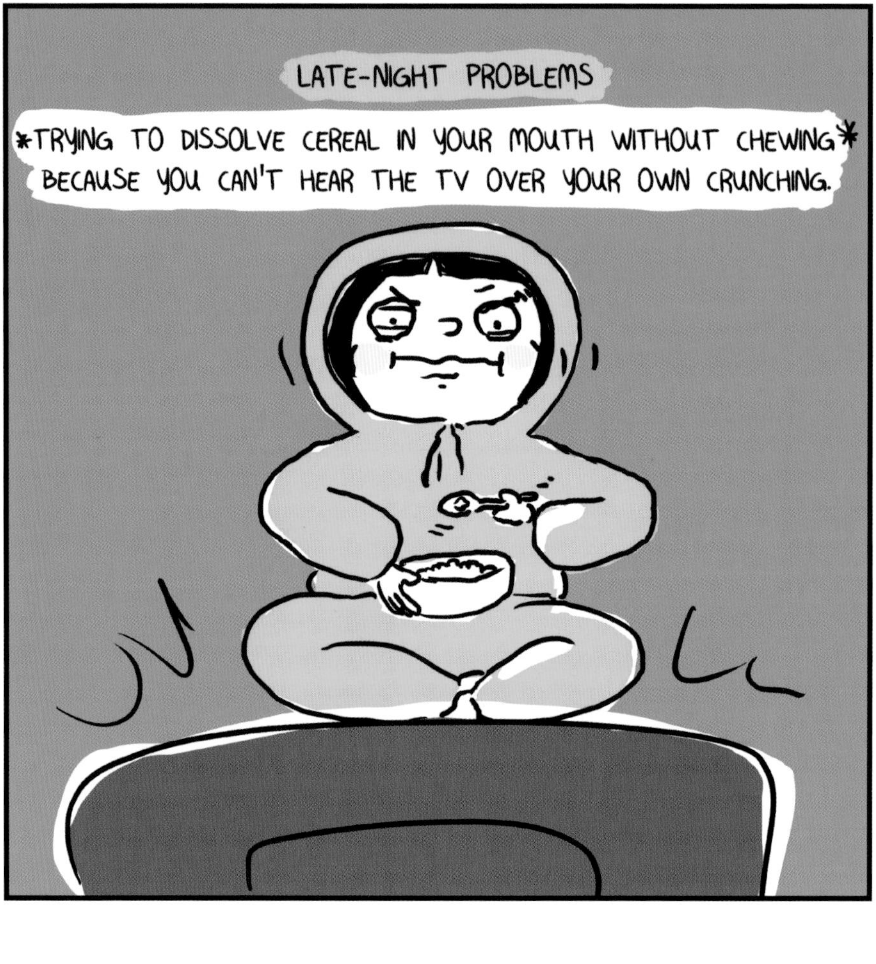
LATE-NIGHT PROBLEMS
TRYING TO DISSOLVE CEREAL IN YOUR MOUTH WITHOUT CHEWING
BECAUSE YOU CAN'T HEAR THE TV OVER YOUR OWN CRUNCHING.

TREAT YOURSELF.

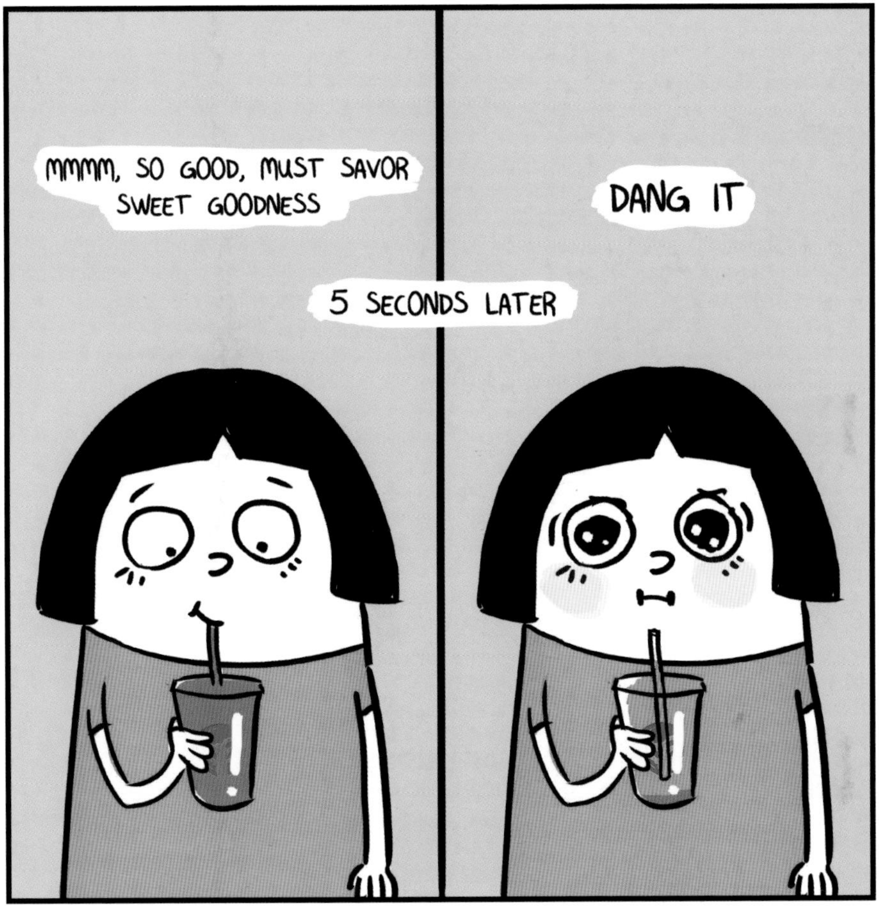
MMMM, SO GOOD, MUST SAVOR SWEET GOODNESS
5 SECONDS LATER
DANG IT

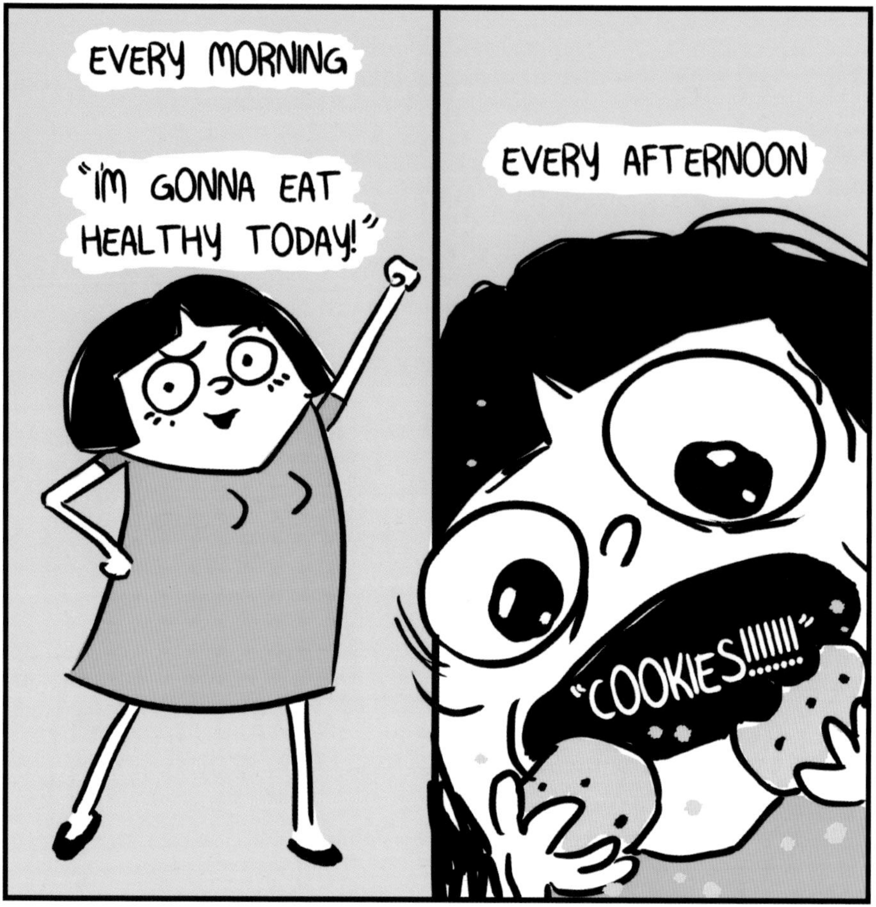
EVERY MORNING
"I'M GONNA EAT HEALTHY TODAY!"
EVERY AFTERNOON
"COOKIES!!!!!!!"

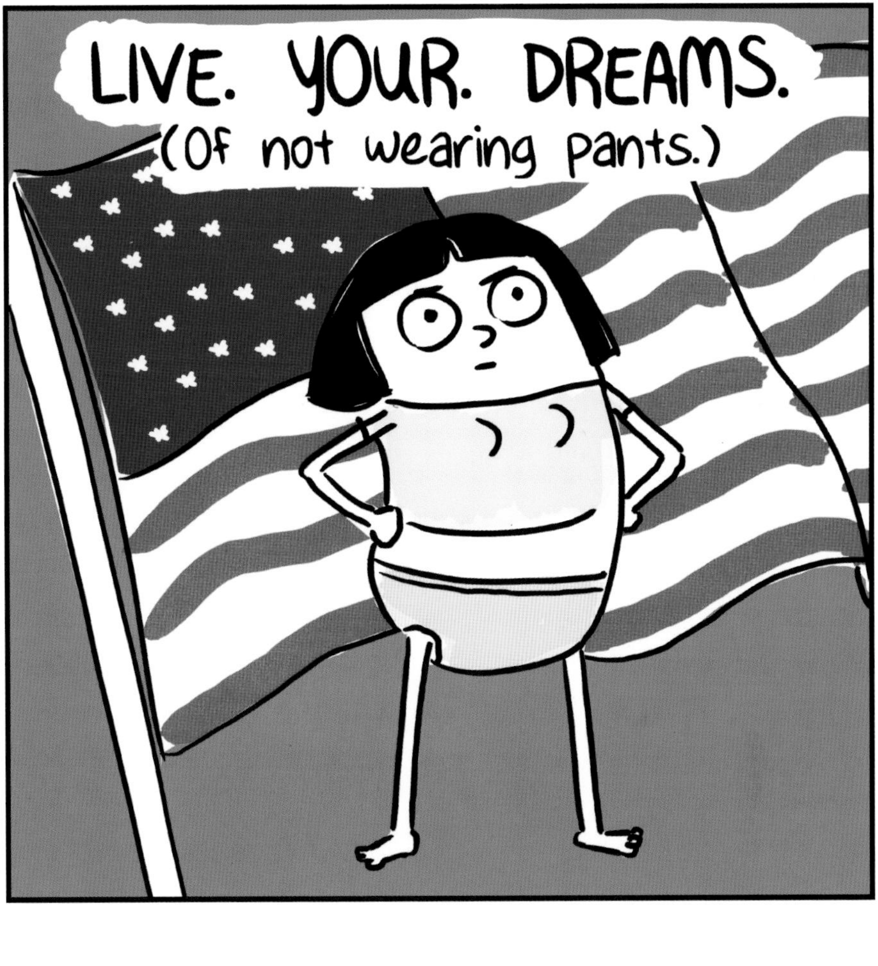
LIVE. YOUR. DREAMS.
(Of not wearing pants.)

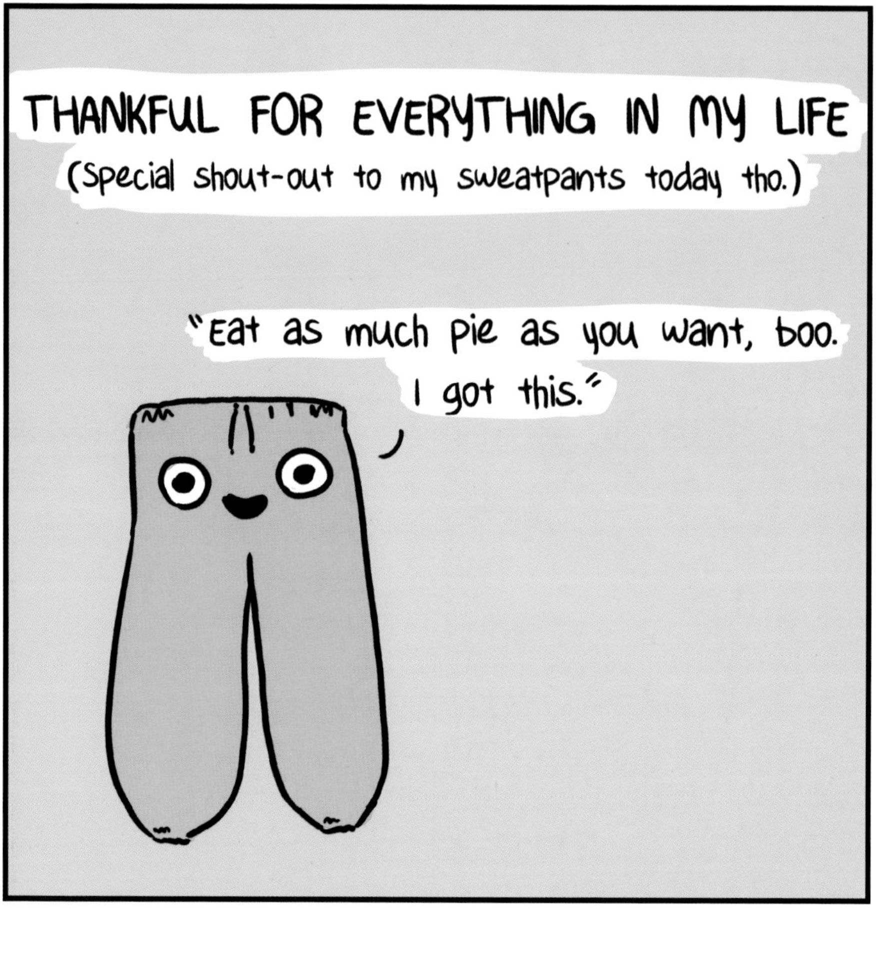
THANKFUL FOR EVERYTHING IN MY LIFE
(Special shout-out to my sweatpants today tho.)
"Eat as much pie as you want, boo.
I got this."

IT'S OK TO BE A HUGE BITCH SOME OR ALL OF THE TIME.

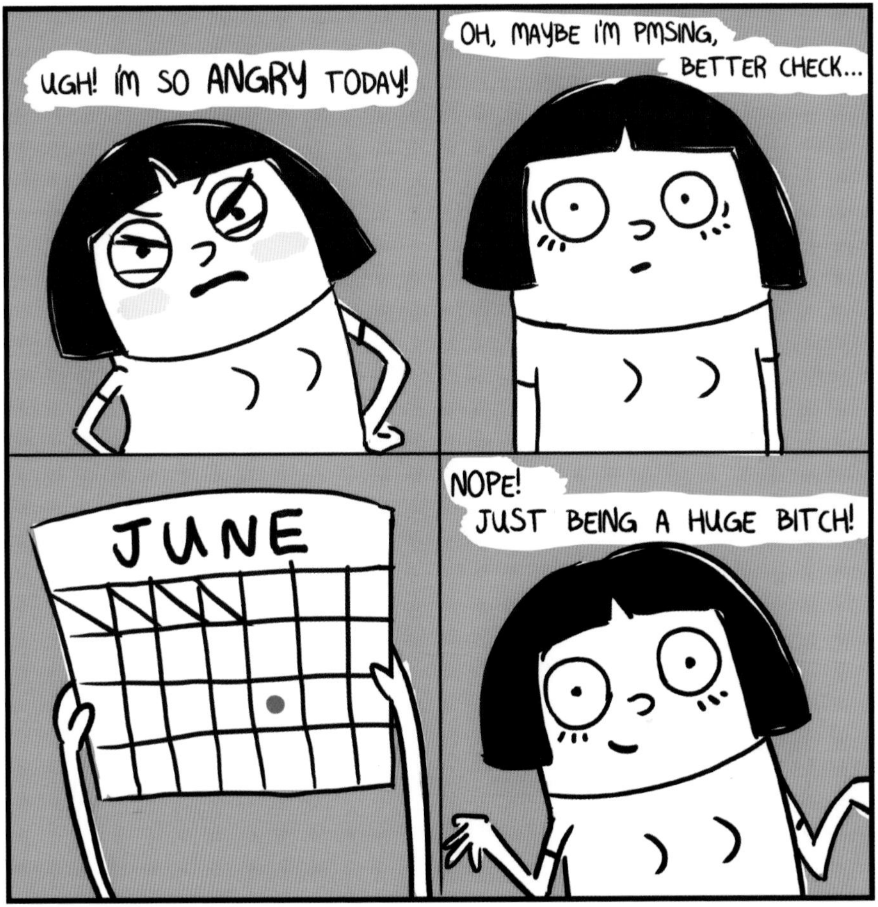
UGH! I'M SO ANGRY TODAY!
OH, MAYBE I'M PMSING,
BETTER CHECK...
JUNE
NOPE!
JUST BEING A HUGE BITCH!

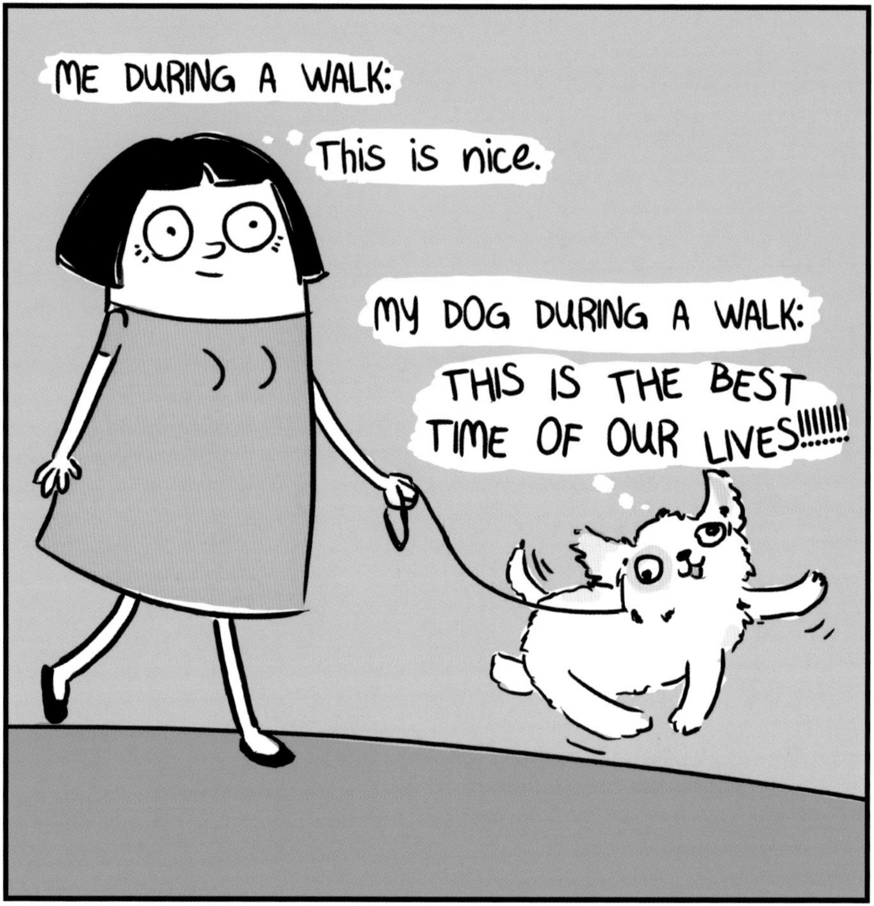
ME DURING A WALK:
This is nice.
MY DOG DURING A WALK:
THIS IS THE BEST TIME OF OUR LIVES!!!!!!!

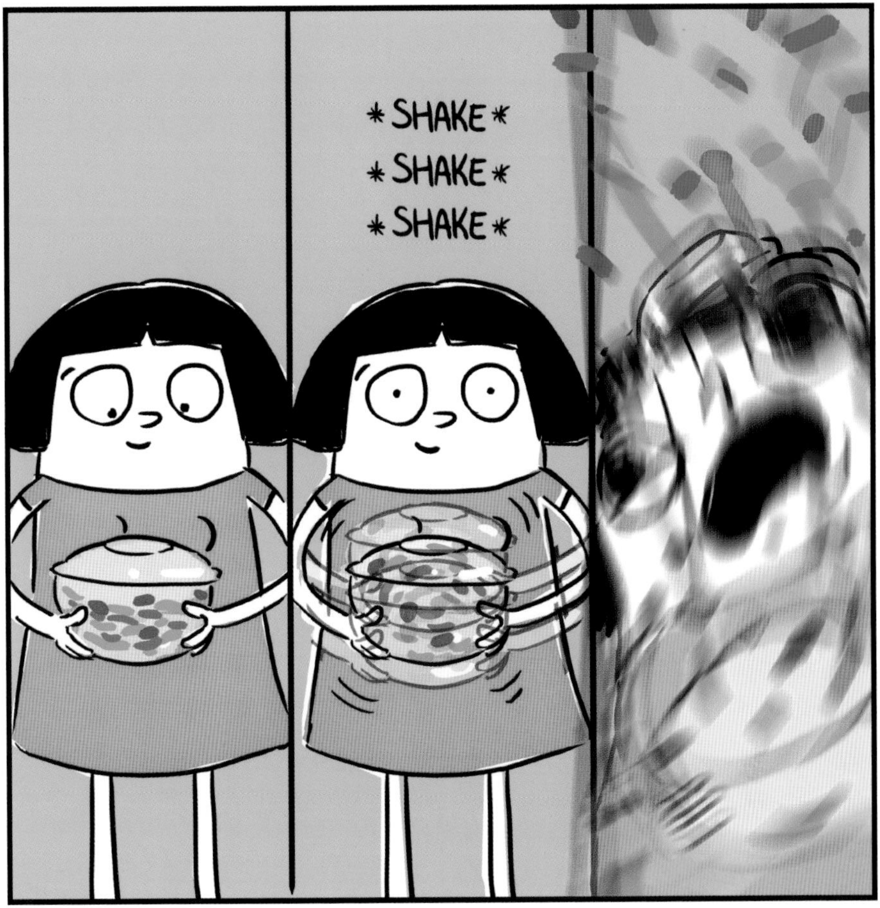
SHAKE
SHAKE
SHAKE

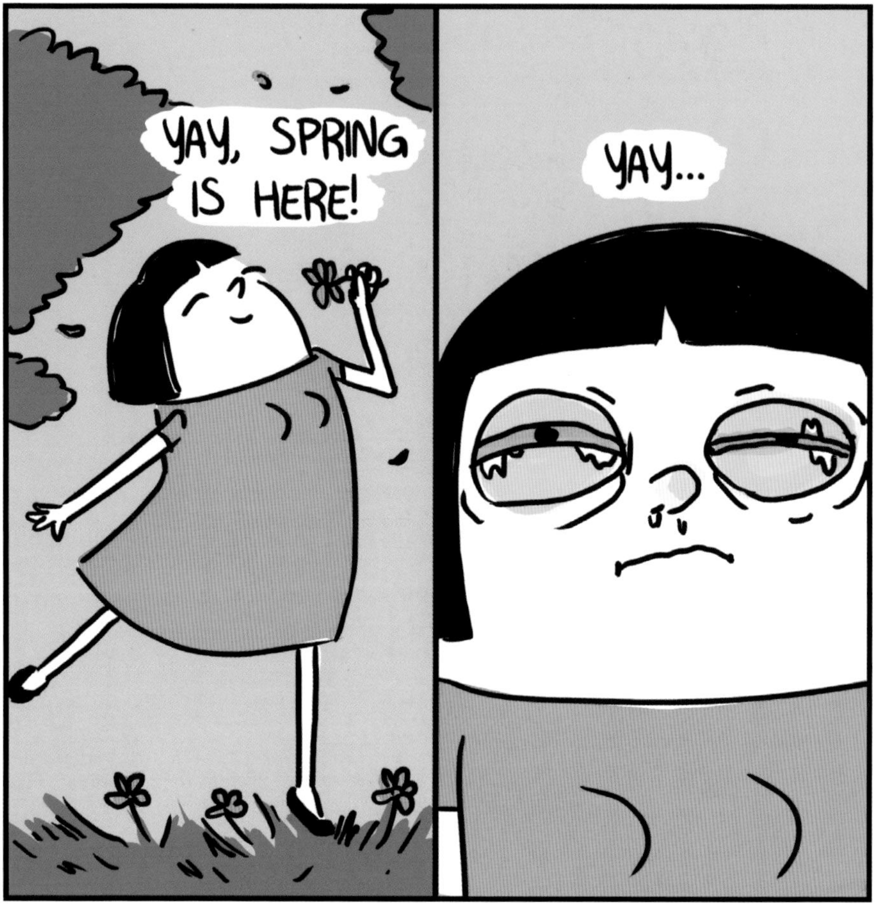
YAY, SPRING IS HERE!
YAY...

WHEN POSSIBLE, ALWAYS CHOOSE SWEATPANTS.

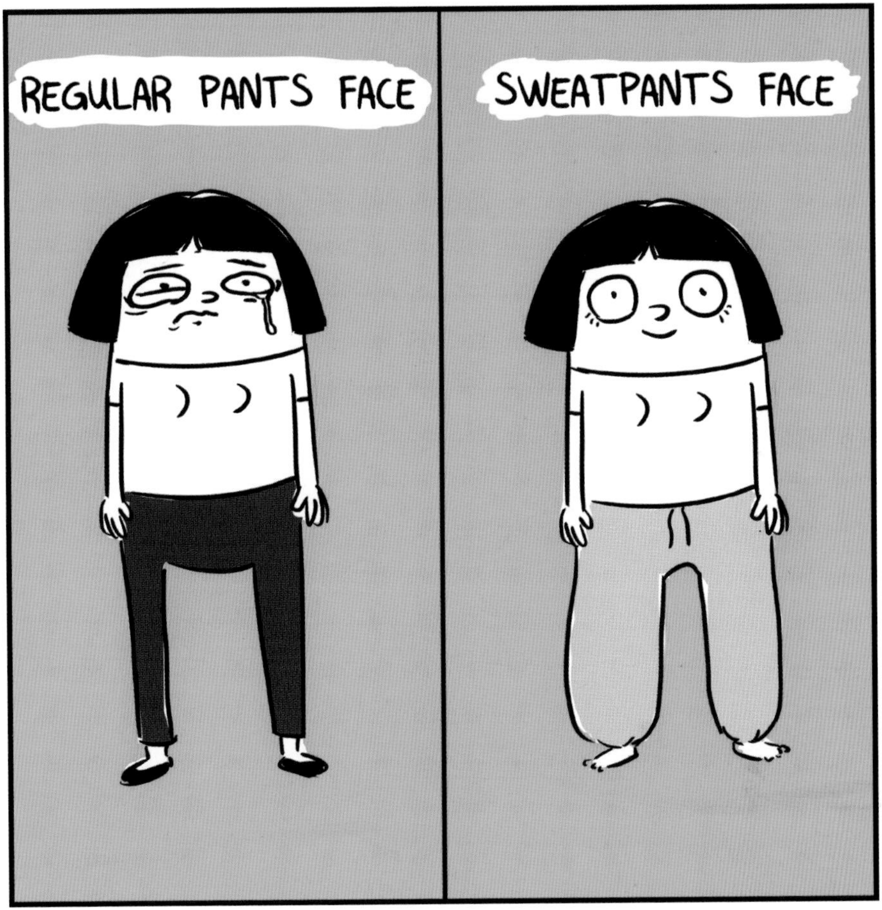
REGULAR PANTS FACE
SWEATPANTS FACE

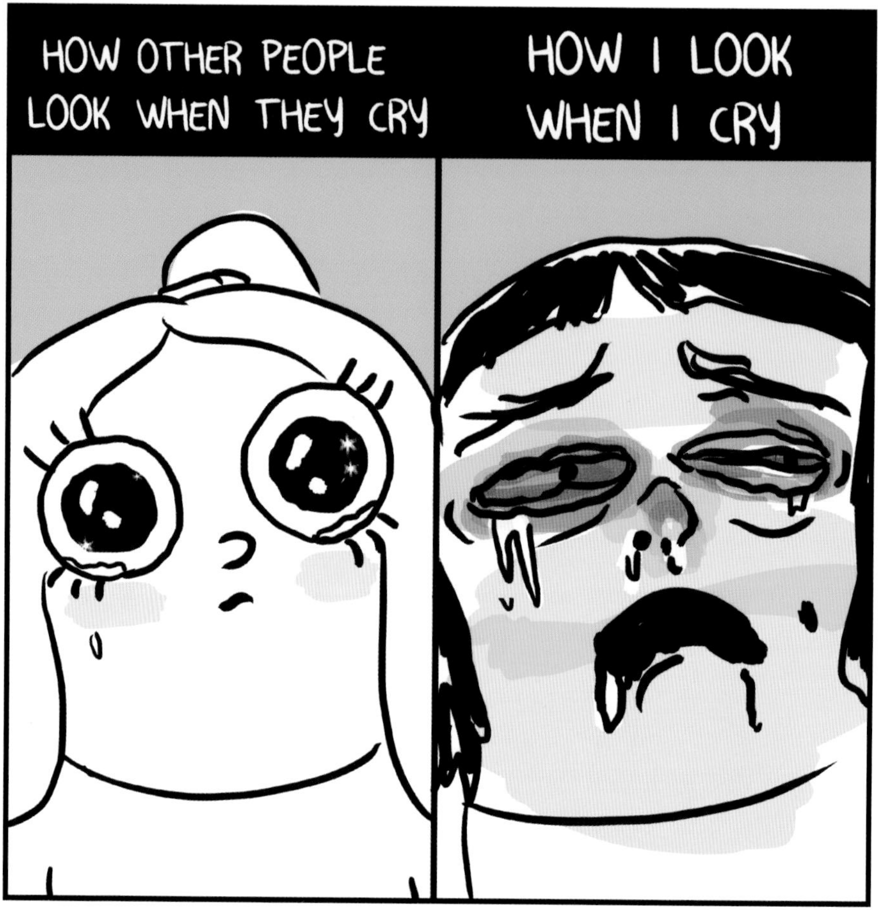
HOW OTHER PEOPLE LOOK WHEN THEY CRY
HOW I LOOK WHEN I CRY

OTHER PEOPLE IN WINTER
BRRR, I'M COLD, WAAAH
ME IN WINTER
Finally!
My natural habitat.

TAKE A MOMENT TO APPRECIATE LIFE'S LITTLE SUCCESSES.

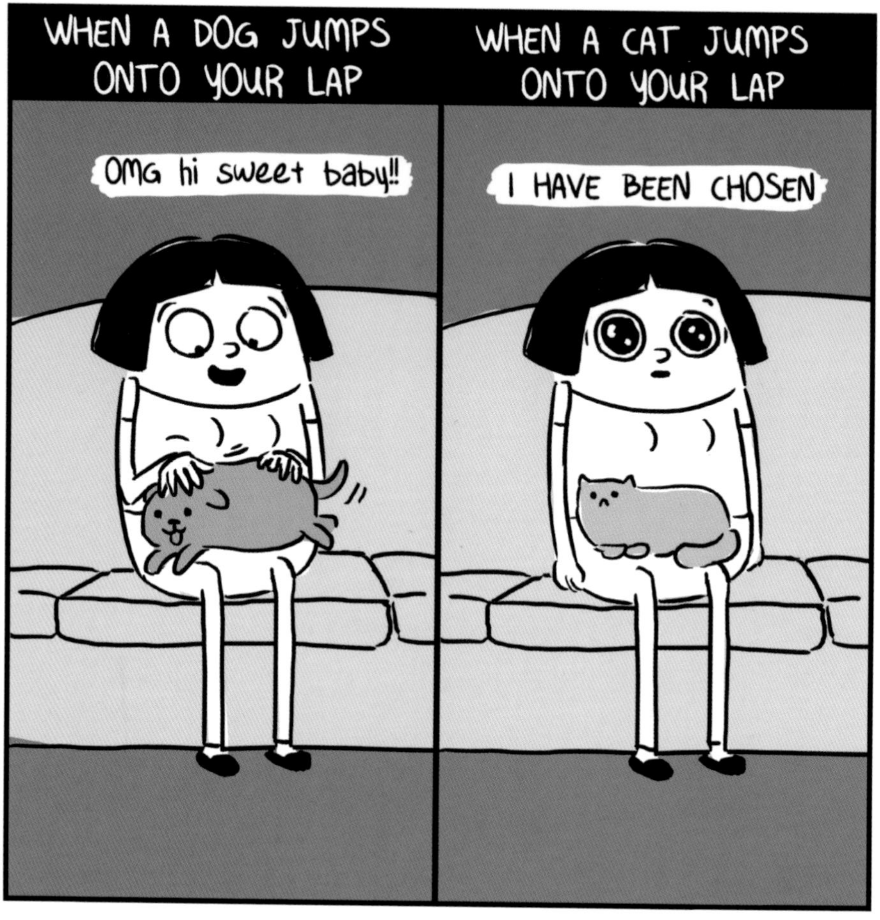
WHEN A DOG JUMPS ONTO YOUR LAP
OMG hi sweet baby!!
WHEN A CAT JUMPS ONTO YOUR LAP
I HAVE BEEN CHOSEN

SOCIAL CONDUCT

ASKING FRIENDS FOR ADVICE IS ALWAYS A GOOD IDEA.

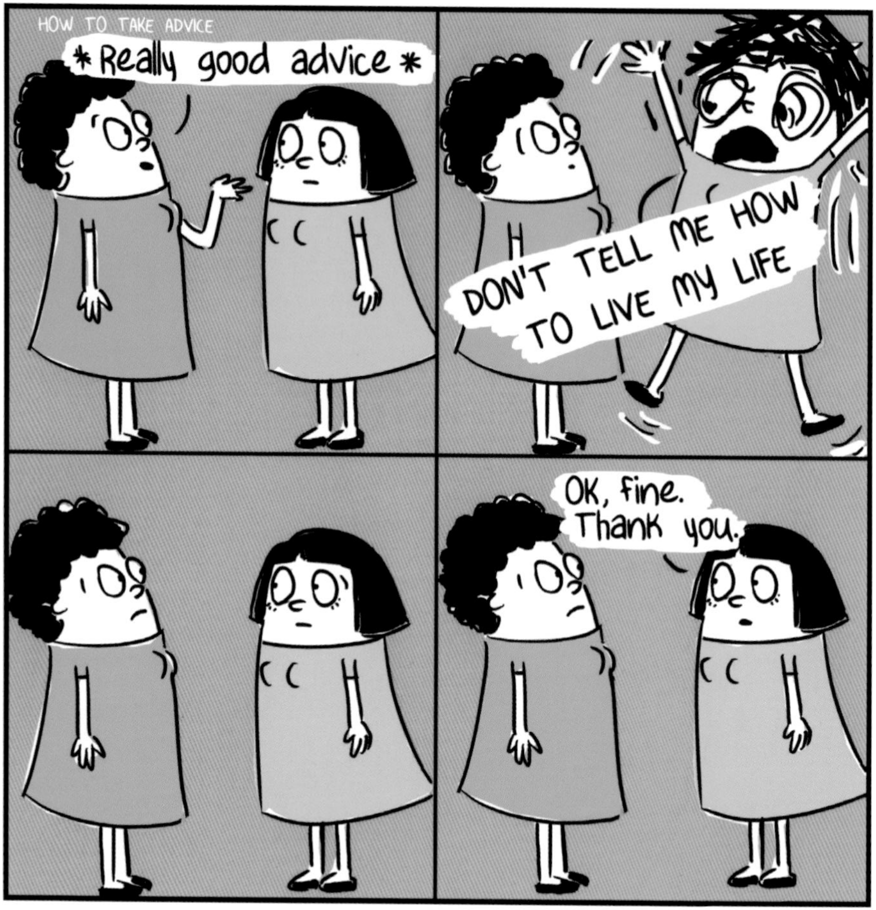
HOW TO TAKE ADVICE
Really good advice
DON'T TELL ME HOW TO LIVE MY LIFE
OK, fine. Thank you.

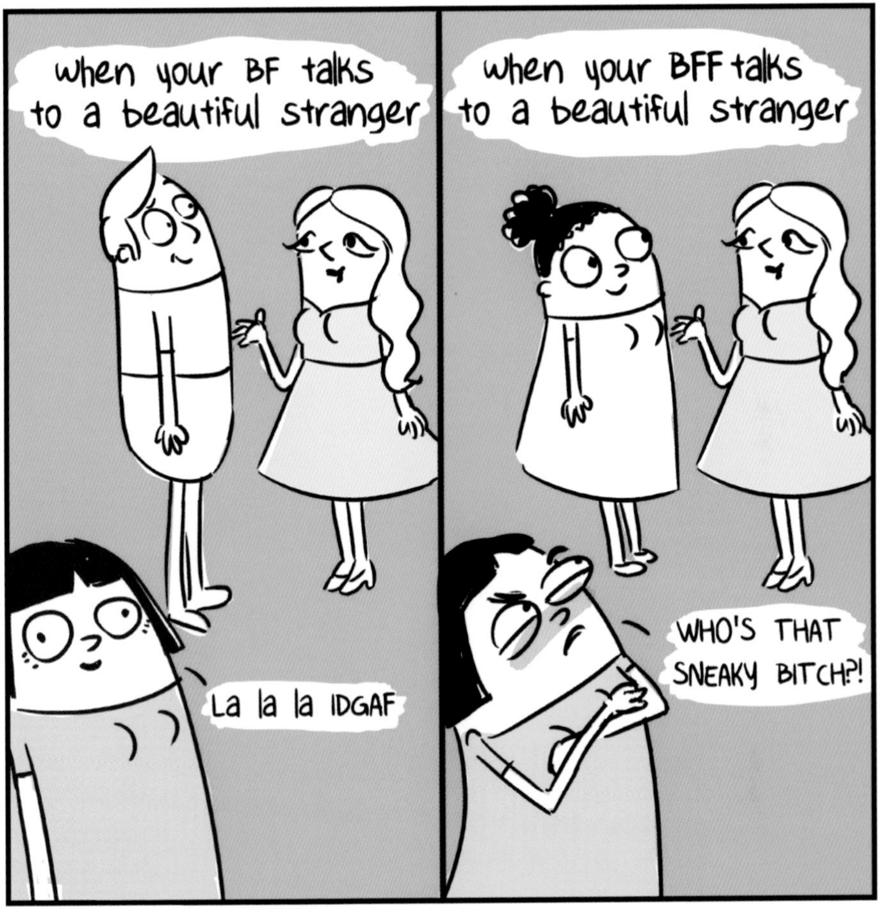
when your BF talks to a beautiful stranger
La la la IDGAF
when your BFF talks to a beautiful stranger
WHO'S THAT SNEAKY BITCH?!

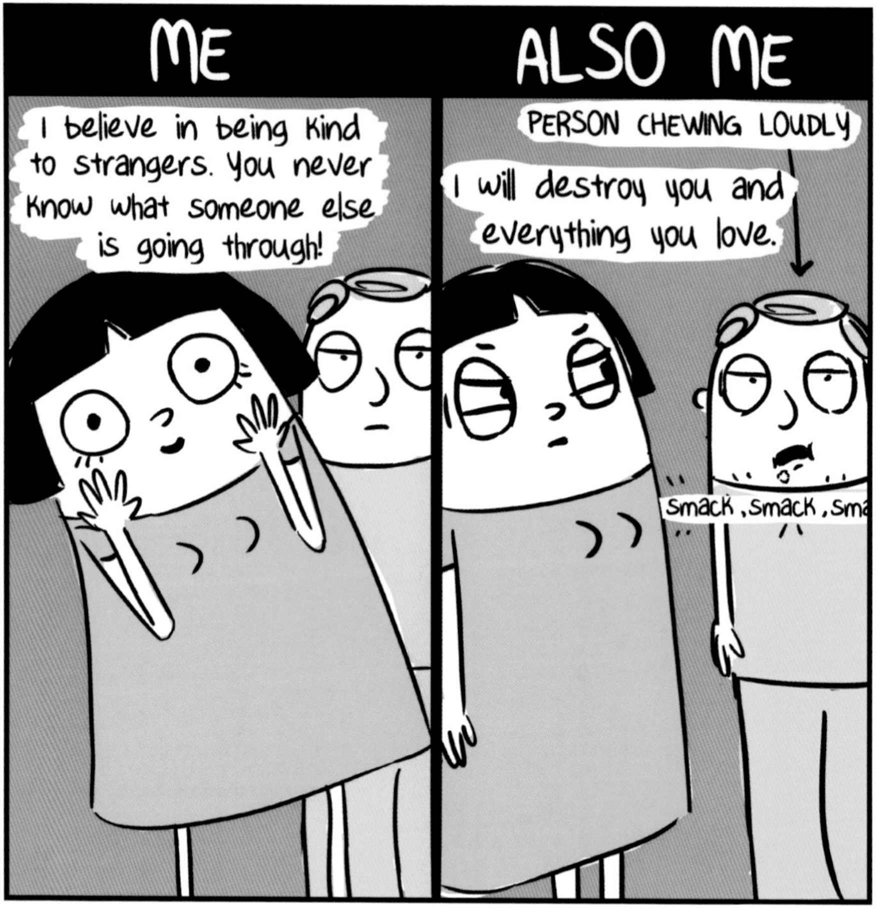
ME
ALSO ME
I believe in being kind to strangers. You never know what someone else is going through!
PERSON CHEWING LOUDLY
I will destroy you and everything you love.
smack, smack, sma

ALWAYS BE PREPARED FOR FALL FESTIVITIES.

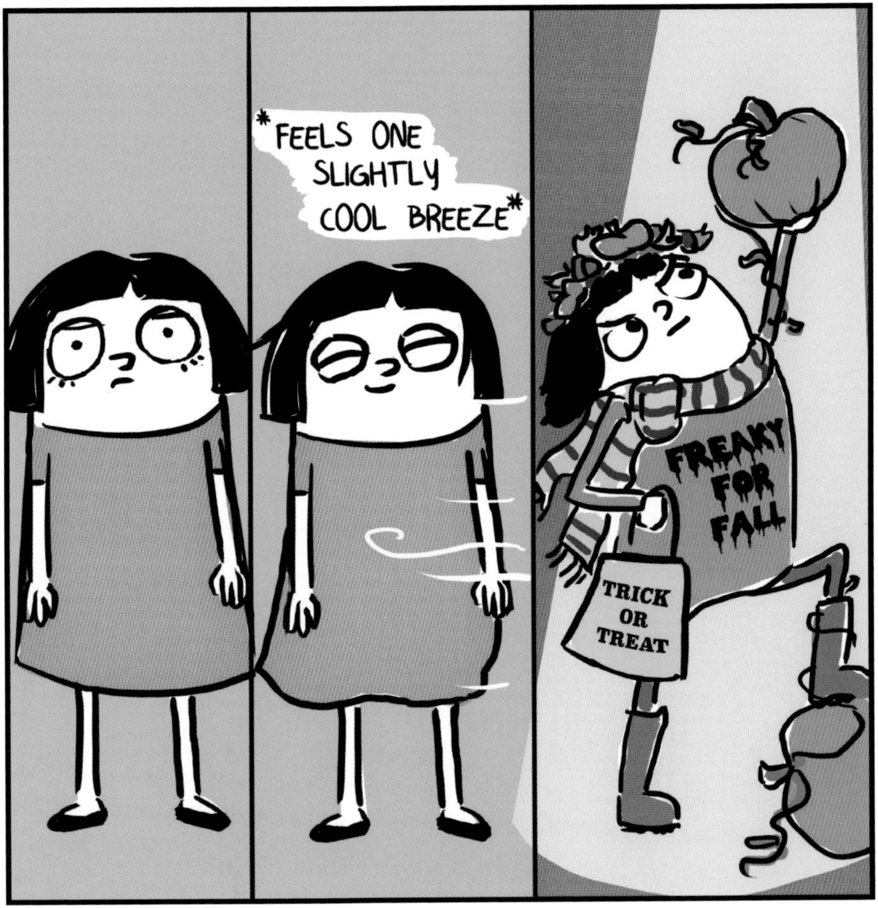
FEELS ONE SLIGHTLY COOL BREEZE
FREAKY FOR FALL
TRICK OR TREAT

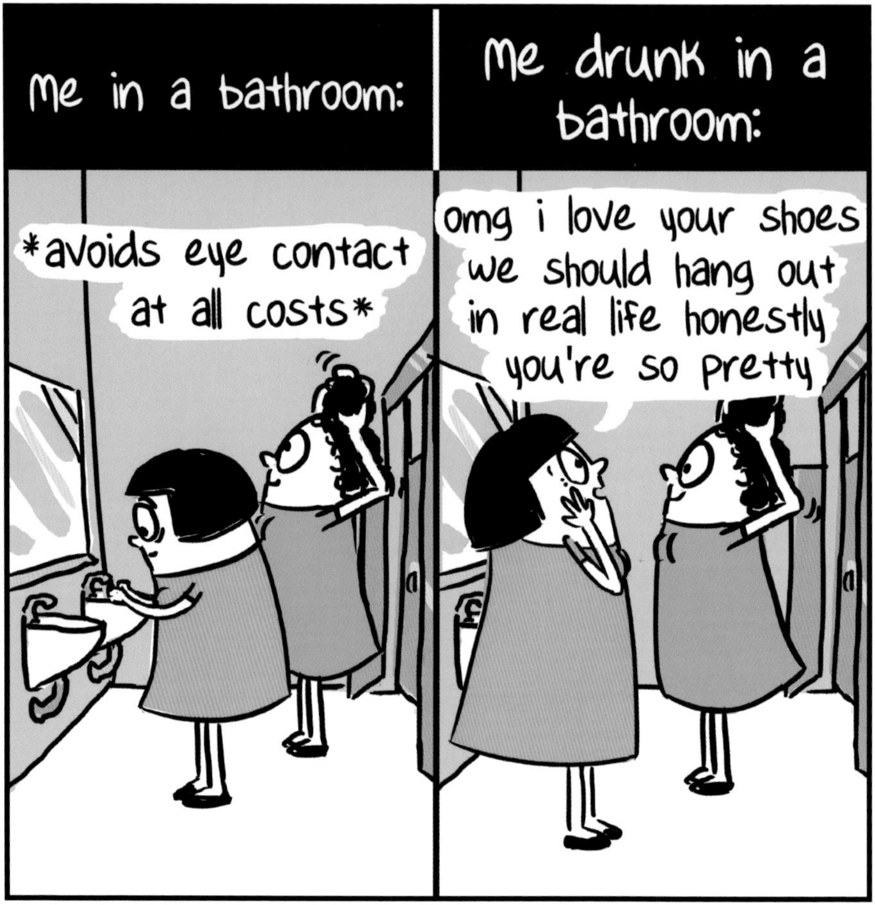
me in a bathroom:
avoids eye contact at all costs
me drunk in a bathroom:
omg i love your shoes we should hang out in real life honestly you're so pretty

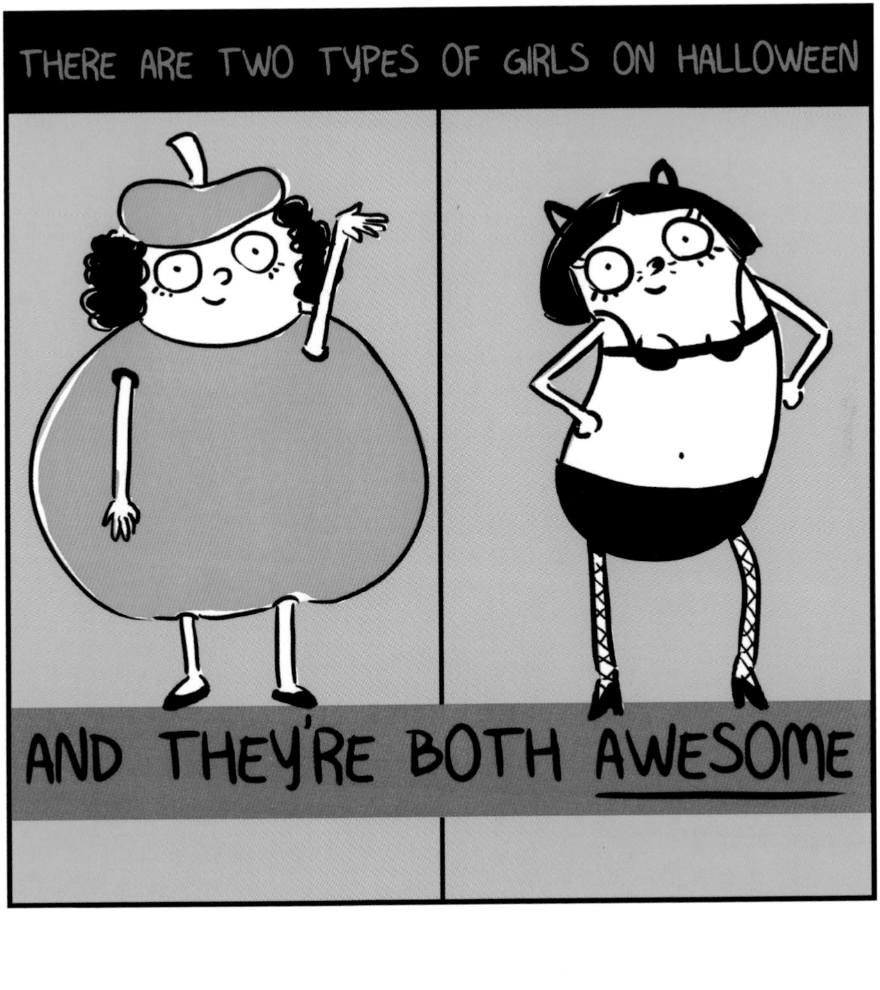
THERE ARE TWO TYPES OF GIRLS ON HALLOWEEN
AND THEY'RE BOTH AWESOME

SEEING YOUR BFF IN YOUR 30s
HOW ARE YOU?
TIRED AND BUSY. YOU?
SAME. SEE YOU AGAIN IN 6 MONTHS?
YEP.

RESPECT YOUR ELDERS.

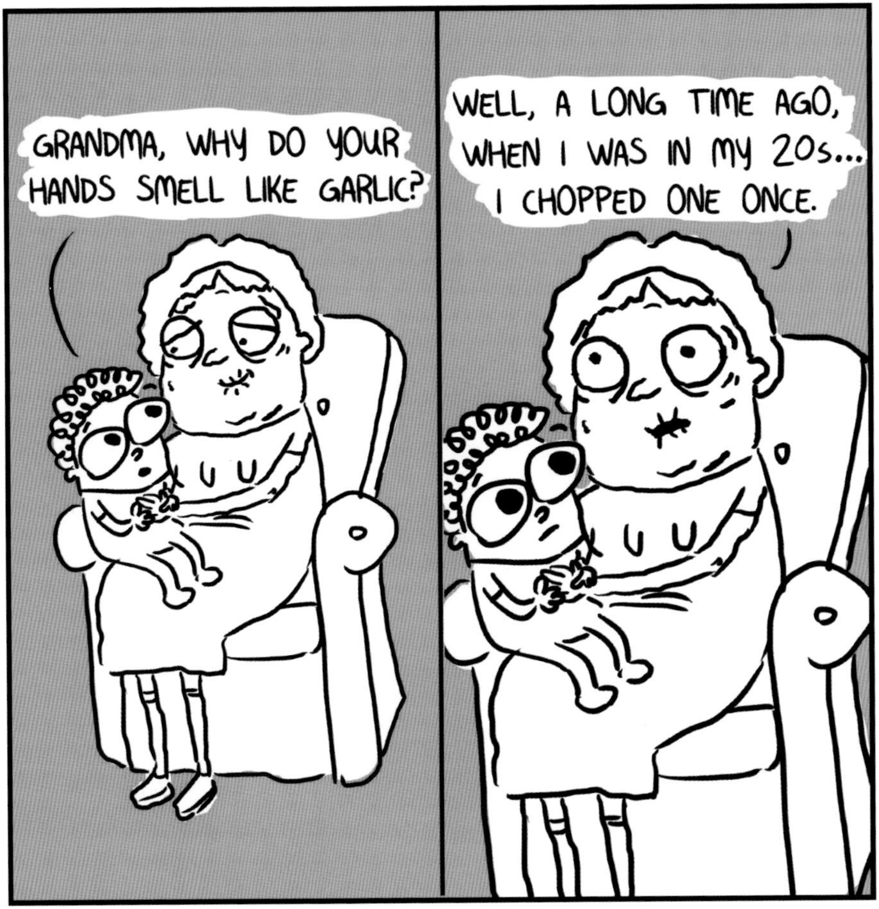
GRANDMA, WHY DO YOUR HANDS SMELL LIKE GARLIC?
WELL, A LONG TIME AGO, WHEN I WAS IN MY 20s... I CHOPPED ONE ONCE.

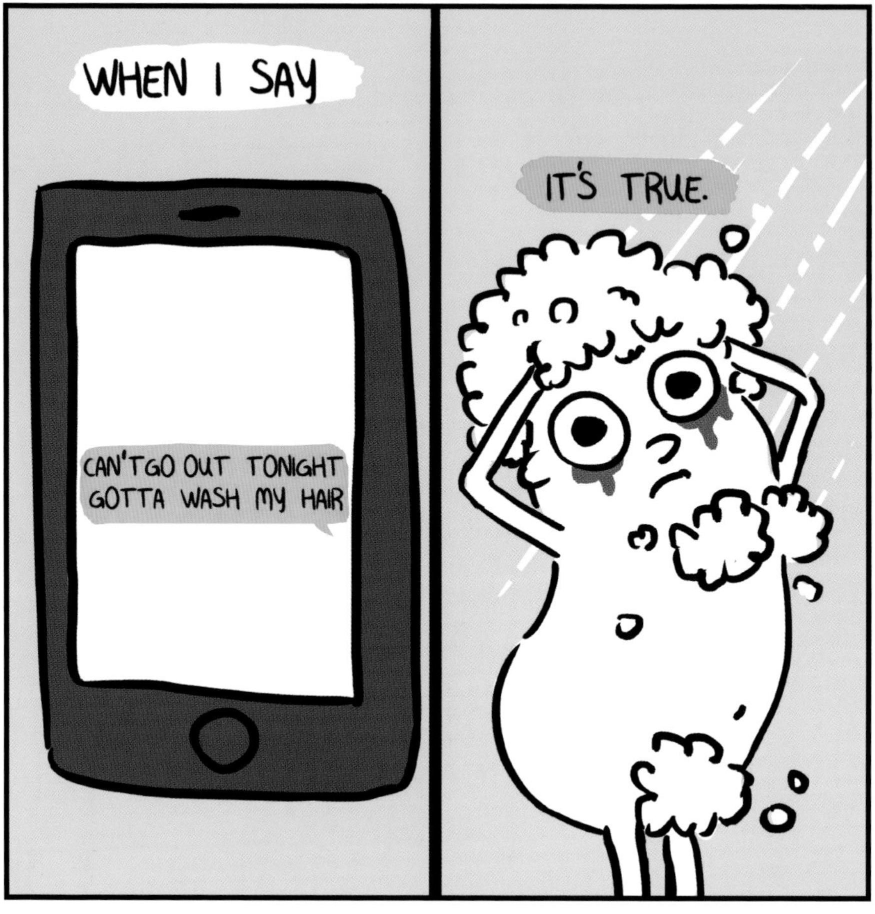
WHEN I SAY
CAN'T GO OUT TONIGHT GOTTA WASH MY HAIR
IT'S TRUE.

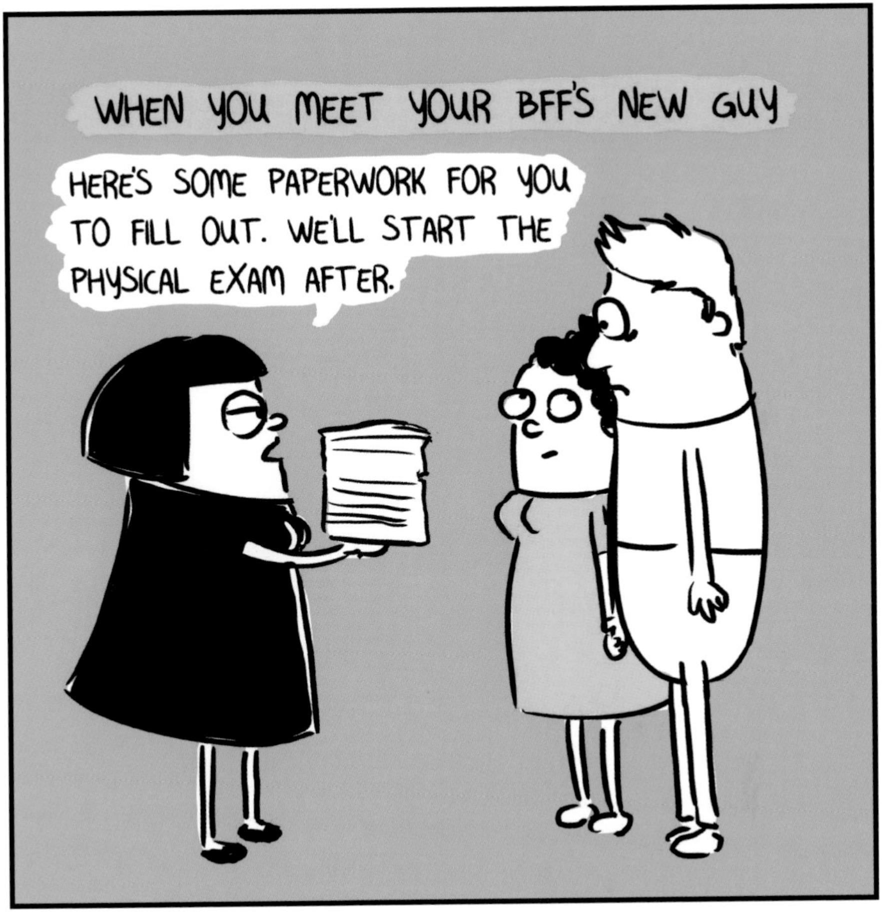
WHEN YOU MEET YOUR BFF'S NEW GUY
HERE'S SOME PAPERWORK FOR YOU TO FILL OUT. WE'LL START THE PHYSICAL EXAM AFTER.

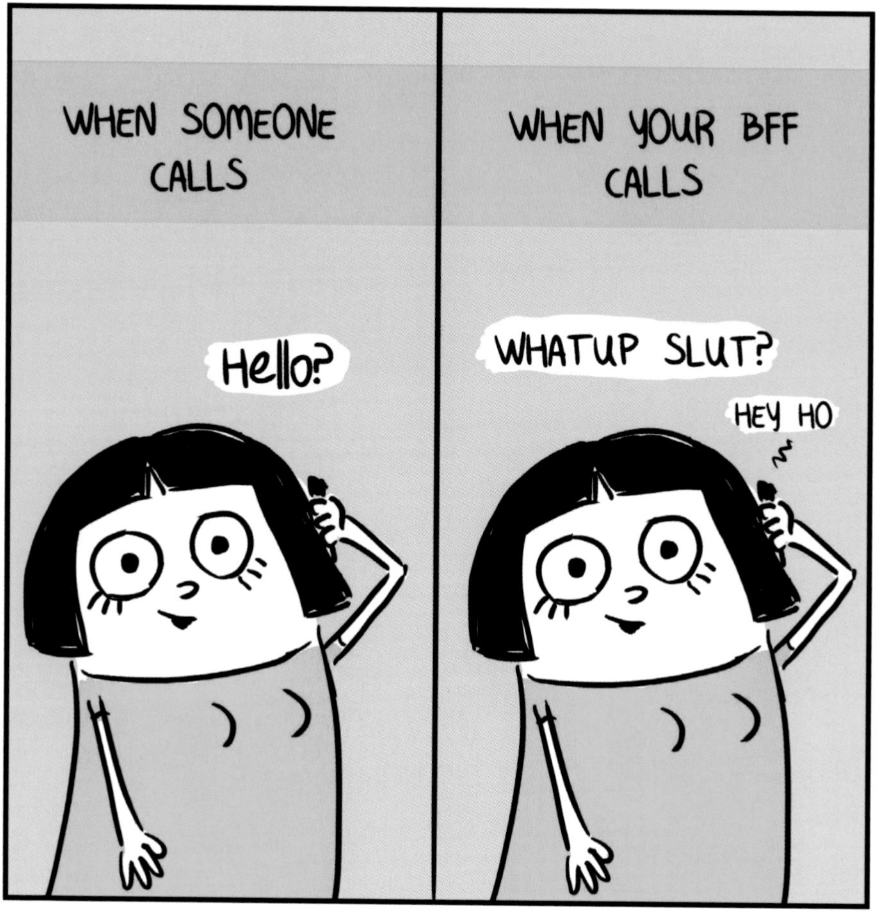
WHEN SOMEONE CALLS
Hello?
WHEN YOUR BFF CALLS
WHATUP SLUT?
HEY HO

MAKING NEW FRIENDS CAN BE HARD.

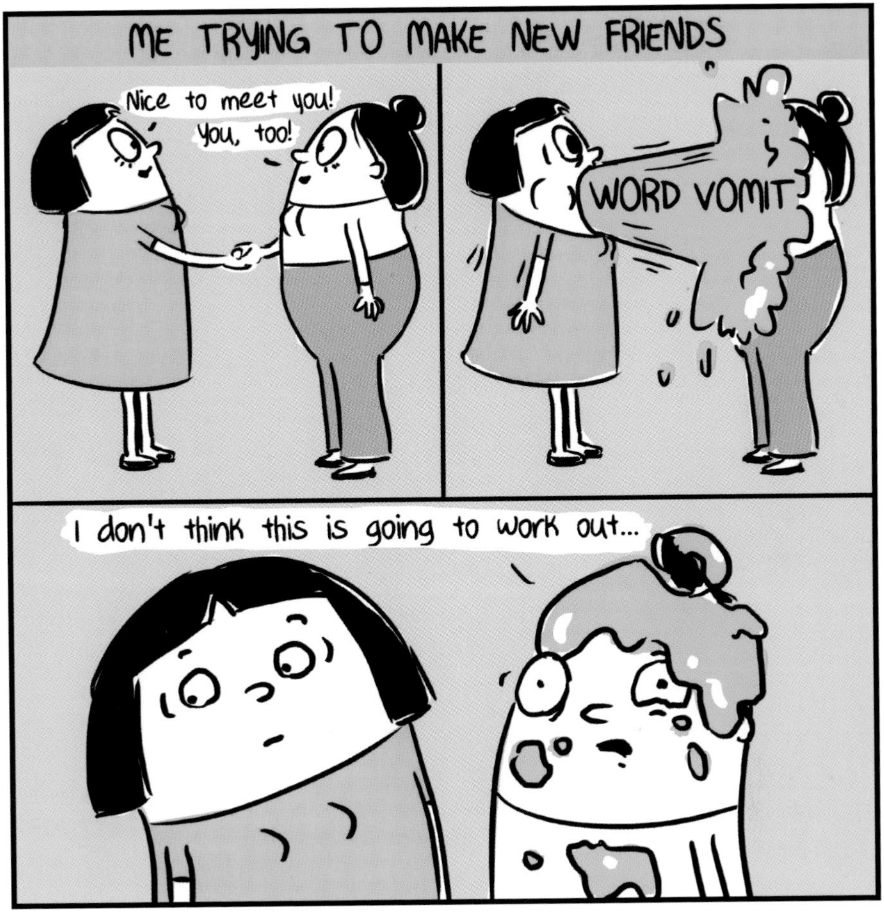
ME TRYING TO MAKE NEW FRIENDS
Nice to meet you!
You, too!
WORD VOMIT
I don't think this is going to work out...

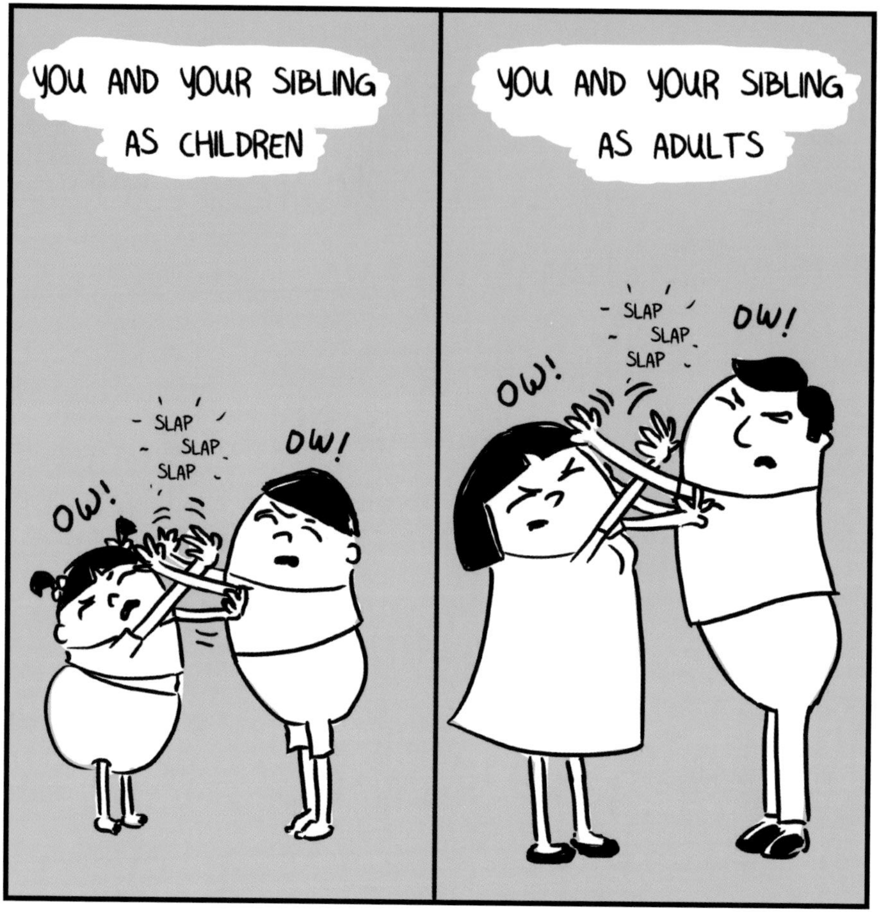
YOU AND YOUR SIBLING AS CHILDREN
SLAP
SLAP
SLAP
OW!
OW!
YOU AND YOUR SIBLING AS ADULTS
SLAP
SLAP
SLAP
OW!
OW!

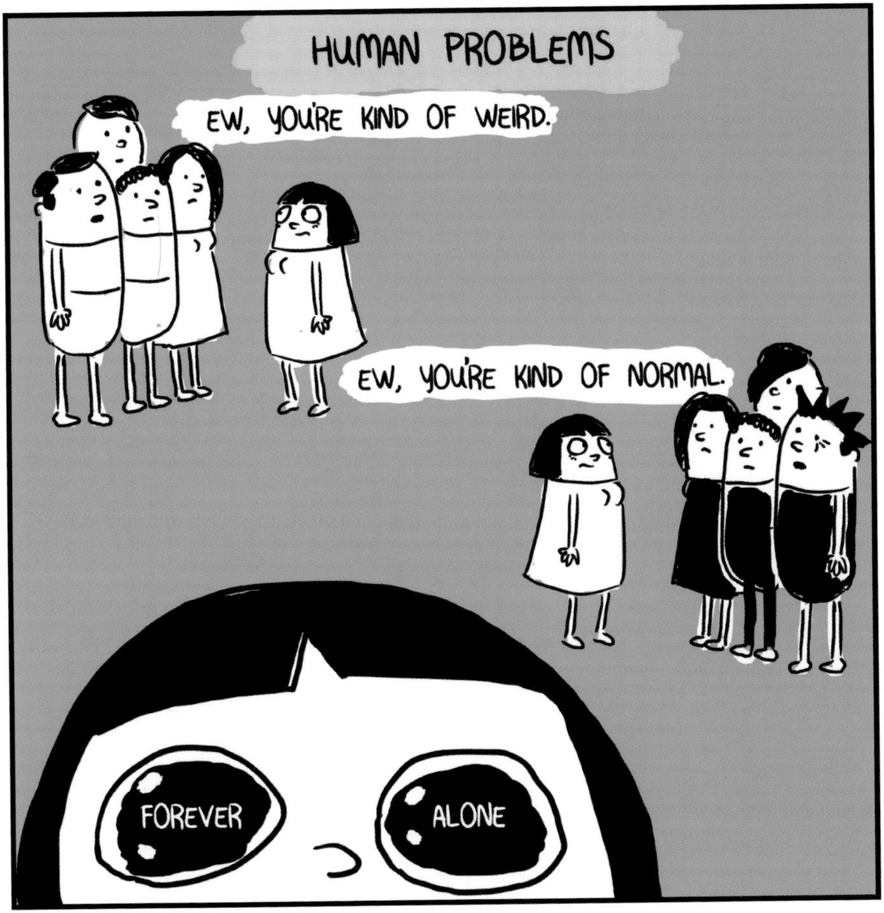
HUMAN PROBLEMS
EW, YOU'RE KIND OF WEIRD.
EW, YOU'RE KIND OF NORMAL.
FOREVER
ALONE

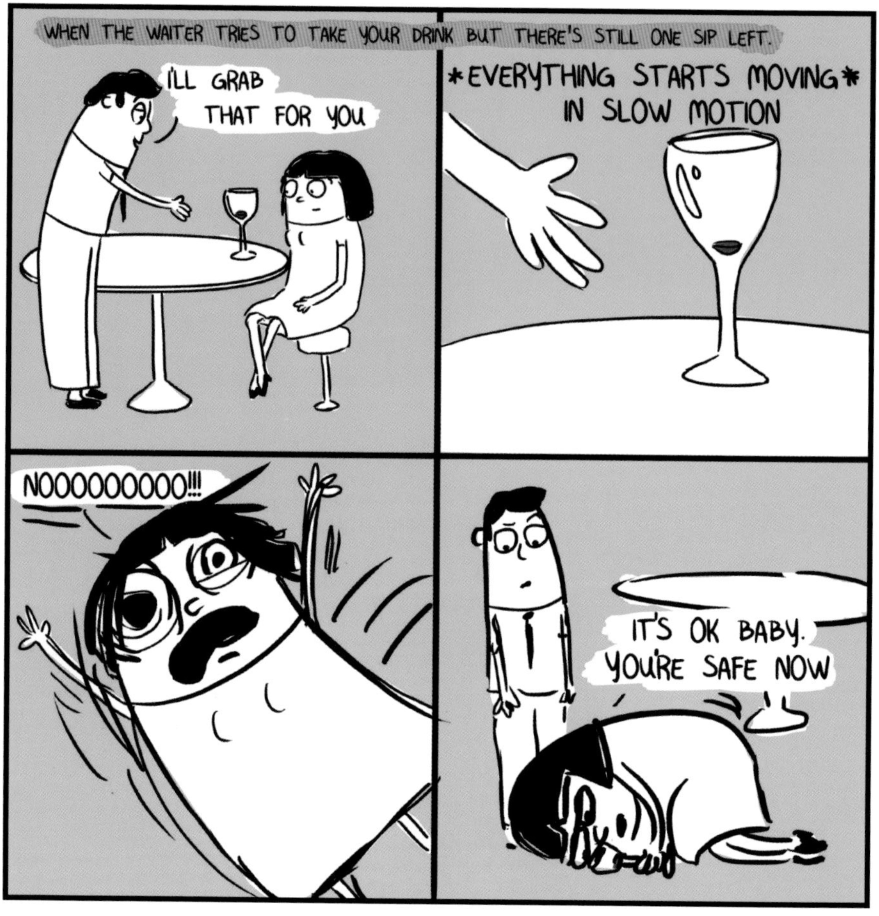
WHEN THE WAITER TRIES TO TAKE YOUR DRINK BUT THERE'S STILL ONE SIP LEFT.
I'LL GRAB THAT FOR YOU
EVERYTHING STARTS MOVING IN SLOW MOTION
NOOOOOOOOO!!!
IT'S OK BABY. YOU'RE SAFE NOW

KARAOKE IS A GREAT WAY TO SOCIALIZE.

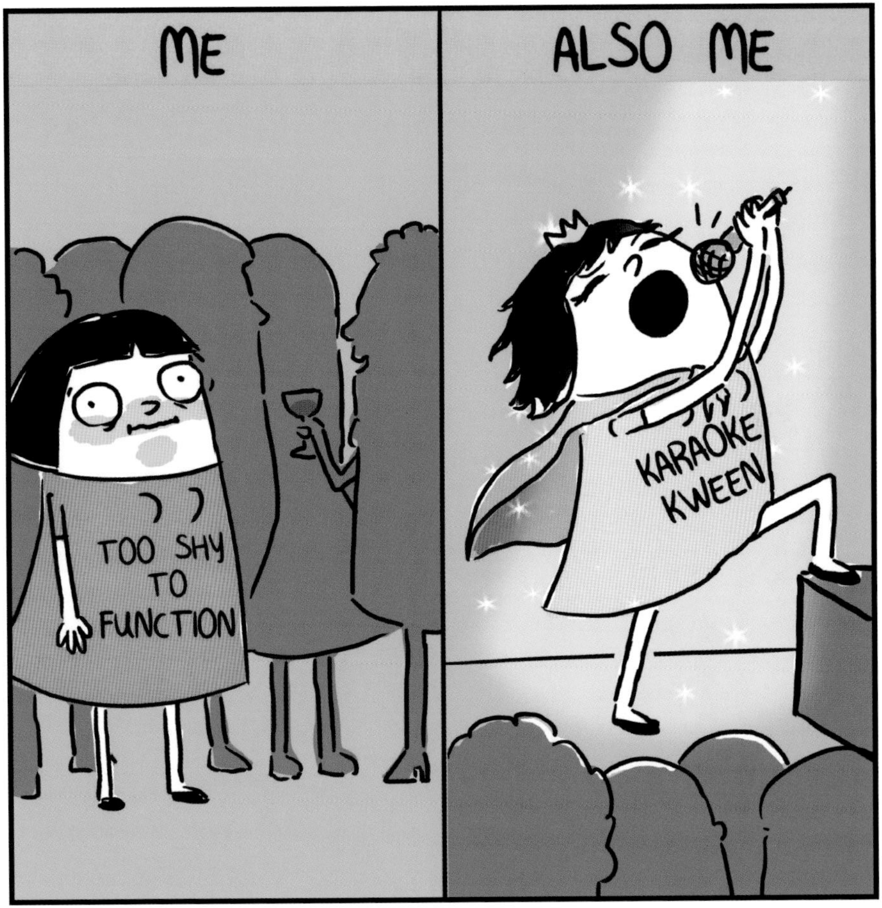
ME
TOO SHY TO FUNCTION
ALSO ME
KARAOKE KWEEN

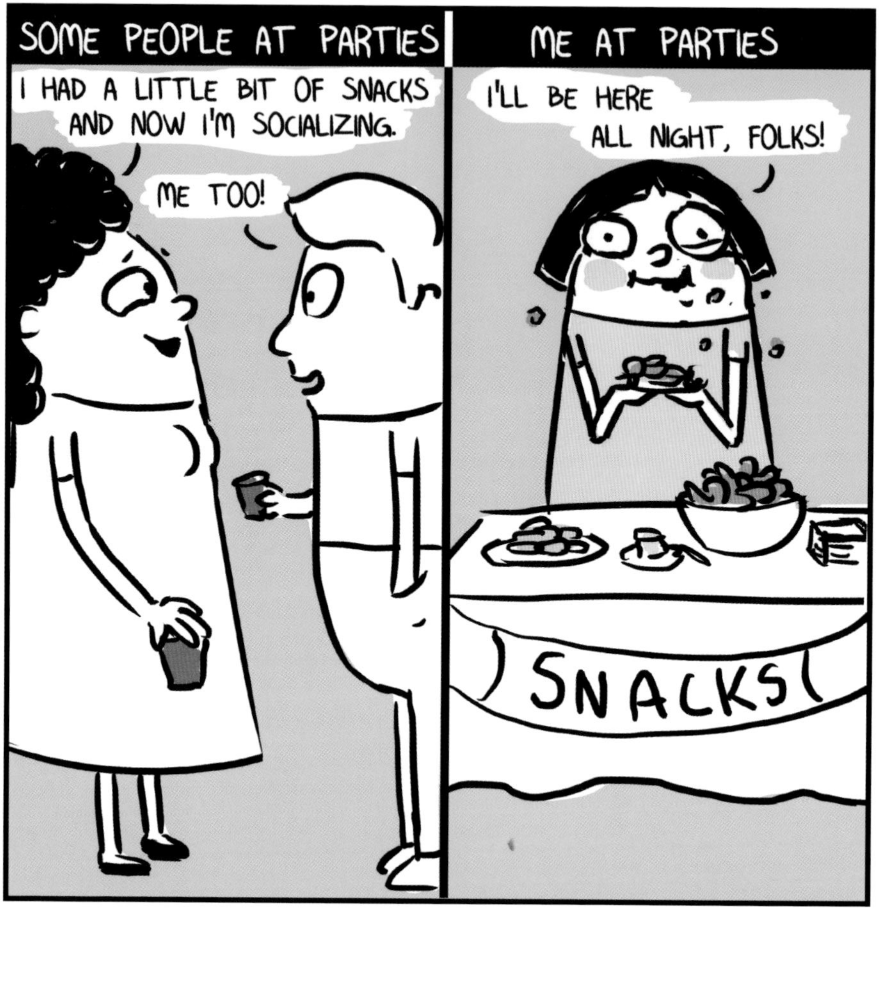
SOME PEOPLE AT PARTIES
I HAD A LITTLE BIT OF SNACKS AND NOW I'M SOCIALIZING.
ME TOO!
ME AT PARTIES
I'LL BE HERE ALL NIGHT, FOLKS!
SNACKS

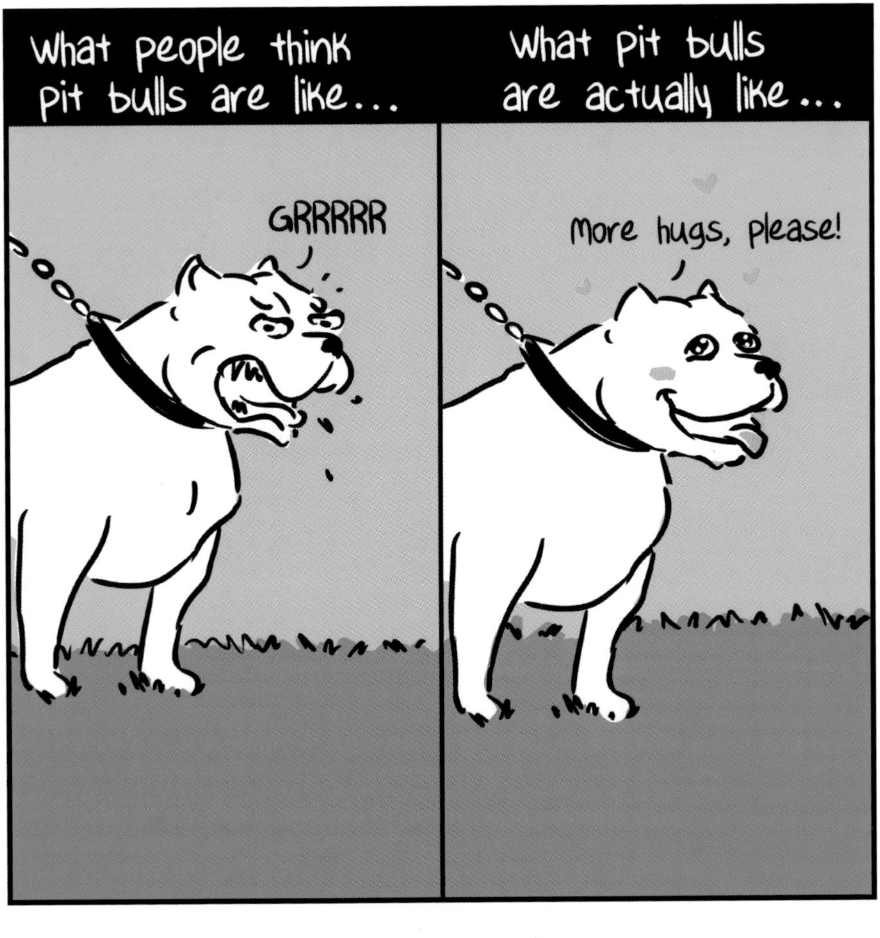
What people think pit bulls are like...
GRRRRR
What pit bulls are actually like...
More hugs, please!

WHEN IN DOUBT, ALWAYS BLAME YOUR SHOE.

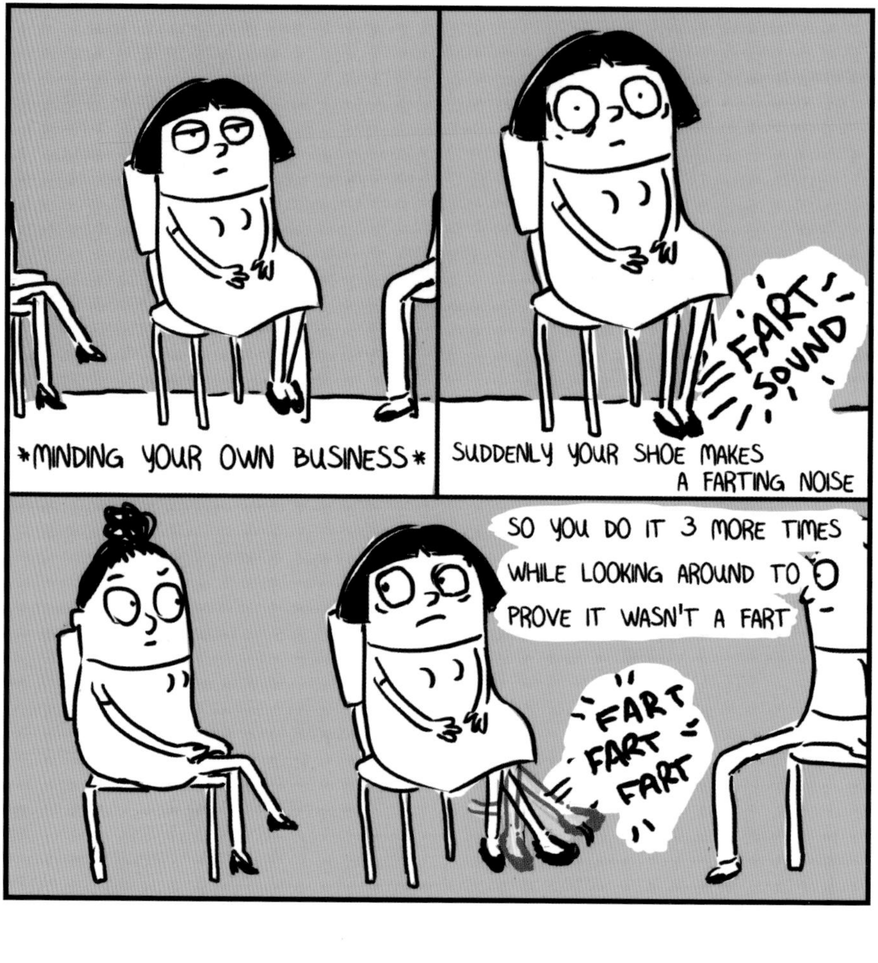

MINDING YOUR OWN BUSINESS
FART SOUND
SUDDENLY YOUR SHOE MAKES A FARTING NOISE
SO YOU DO IT 3 MORE TIMES WHILE LOOKING AROUND TO PROVE IT WASN'T A FART
FART FART FART